Contents

Preface

I am currently on a mission. My mission is to help transform the way most teachers approach classroom management. The old ways of using anger and intimidation to discipline students are no longer effective, and our students are paying the price. A new era of student behavior demands a New Style of classroom management for teachers—one where organization, fairness, and clarity are the basis, not fear and intimidation. My goal is that teachers everywhere will learn to drastically lower the stress that accompanies poor management skills and unlock their gifts of teaching. I want to save our teachers and our schools from falling apart because of the unsuccessful classroom management techniques being used in many places.

I had two main inspirations for beginning my study of classroom management. First, my study began a few years ago when I had three straight terms teaching a class that made me want to quit because of their misbehavior. The interesting thing about these classes is that there was very little extreme misbehavior taking place. There were no threats, no fights, and no weapons taken out. These classes simply had a high frequency of more simple misbehaviors. I tried to use intimidation and meanness to put a stop to the misbehavior, but this just caused me stress and had little effect on the students' behavior anyway. I explored and experimented until I eventually developed the plan for classroom management that is described in this book. The plan worked so well for me and for other teachers at my school that some of them encouraged me to write a book about my experiences.

My second inspiration for the book may be surprising. It comes from one of my favorite television shows, *Supernanny*. I have never had kids of my own, but I love this show. I have always been fascinated by discipline, whether in the classroom or in the home. The star of the show is Jo Frost, who goes into homes that are in a state of chaos because of out-of-control children. She observes the families and comes up with sensible discipline plans for them. The results are astounding, as the parents learn how to successfully bring order to their homes. What she does is not rocket science; she just teaches the families how to create an organized discipline plan.

After discovering *Supernanny*, I thought to myself, "Wouldn't it be great if someone could do the same thing that she does for families, but in classrooms instead?" My goal is to help totally transform the way teachers handle student behavior problems, either as a result of reading this book, or through individual training to help teachers develop effective discipline plans.

The main objective for this book is not to turn teachers into great disciplinarians, although that can be a benefit of using the strategies being taught. The ultimate goal is to help teachers whose gifts for teaching are being hindered because of their inability to successfully manage classroom behavior. Maybe I can even help you.

Happy teaching,
Campbell (the Discipline Doctor)

Introduction

Why a Different Approach Is Needed

To Be (a Witch), or Not to Be,
That Is the Question

There are many more people with a gift for teaching
than there are with a gift for classroom management.

—Doug Campbell

Early Days

"And we would like to say good-bye to Doug Campbell. He
did a good job for us, had some problems with classroom discipline . . ."

Ugh. I cringed as I heard my principal saying those words
at the faculty meeting at the end of my second year as a high
school teacher. It was the spring of 1997, and I was leaving my
job teaching social studies in South Carolina to teach math in
North Carolina. How embarrassing. I did not consider myself
weak in the area of classroom management, but it was definitely
not a strength of mine at this stage of my career. I actually had
only one mild incident of student misbehavior that year that

Paraphrased from William Shakespeare's *Hamlet*.

involved the principal, but it was enough for him to associate me with having a problem.

The principal was right, though. Classroom management was a weakness of mine. Yes, I did have other skills that were necessary for successful teaching, but this was definitely not one of them. After completing my secondary teacher certification and being halfway through a master's degree in education, this glaring weakness still existed. Despite all of that training, I had had very little actual instruction in how to manage a classroom. I knew that there had to be a way to solve this great mystery. Twelve years would pass before I found any significant answers.

The Revelation Comes

Not long into my teaching career I made a comforting discovery. I found that I was not the only teacher having difficulty with classroom management. Everywhere I looked, teachers were facing the same challenges in their classrooms, many with unsuccessful results. Almost every teacher that I knew had some issue with student misbehavior. It did not matter what grade they were teaching, where they lived, or how wealthy the families were in the communities they taught. The challenges were the same.

Of course, the severity of the problems that some teachers face is different from others, but the basic issues are the same everywhere. The main concern of most teachers comes down to one issue: "How do I handle student misbehaviors in my classroom?"

Most teachers know how to handle the extreme misbehaviors, like swearing, fighting, stealing, using drugs, and so on. There are clear protocols in place in most schools for handling these kinds of situations.

But what about smaller issues like sleeping in class, excessive talking, and students getting out of their desks without permission? These minor misbehaviors can be much more disruptive and stressful for a teacher than the extreme issues. Why? Because most teachers do not have an effective plan in place ahead of time to handle them. As a result, teachers are forced to react on the spot without a prepared response.

---

*Each chapter will include a feature called "Old School/New School." The **Old School** portion will describe a traditional strategy or idea about classroom management that is now outdated. The **New School** part will explain the new and improved approach.*

Old School: Good teachers have natural gifts for teaching as well as for classroom management.

New School: Good teachers have natural gifts for teaching their subject but may not have natural gifts for classroom management.

Despite what may be shown on television or in the movies, most teachers are not primarily worried by the possibility of drugs or violence at their school. They are more concerned about the feeling of not being able to handle the *smaller* disruptions that take place in classrooms every day. Without a plan in place, the result is a mismanaged classroom, resentful students, and a stressed out teacher.

Top Concerns of School Teachers on Any Given Class Day

- Will I have enough activities to occupy my students for an entire period?
- Will my teaching be interesting and stimulating?
- Will I know everything that I need to know?
- Will my students learn?
- Will my students like me?
- *Will my classes behave well?*

The unfortunate reality is that most teachers are left on their own to handle these kinds of problems. As I was, they are "thrown into the fire" and expected to be able to handle these difficult circumstances with very little training. This is why I am writing this book. I am going to uncover the secrets of dealing with these situations to help teachers everywhere master the seemingly elusive skills of classroom management.

All teachers have natural abilities. Some have the gift of subject knowledge in math, science, language, social studies, and so forth. Others have a gift for public speaking and being entertaining. And a select few teachers have a talent for classroom management. This skill was not something that these teachers formally learned; the ability just came naturally to them. These people run their classes so smoothly that they seem to have been born to teach. The students do exactly what they are supposed to do, and they rarely, if ever, give the teacher a problem.

In most cases these gifted teachers did not have any more training than the rest of us. What I did not realize early on, though, was that this natural talent was not nearly as common as I thought. In fact, I found out that most teachers do *not* have the gift for classroom management. Many of them would actually be tremendous teachers if they could only figure out a way to successfully manage classroom behavior. I discovered that many teachers have great skill within their subjects, but at the same time have unsatisfactory skills for controlling their classrooms. What an encouraging discovery. I was not alone!

At the beginning of my teaching career, I quickly learned that my own management skills were average at best. I felt comfortable in the classroom, but there were a lot of situations that I did not feel equipped to handle. Even before I began teaching, I knew that my best skills were explaining math and relating to young people. Unfortunately, while these gifts could take me a long way in teaching, there was still something missing.

Need for a Change

I developed an interest in classroom management and discipline early on, probably as a result of my struggles as a first year teacher. I admit that I was jealous of the teachers who had a gift in this area. I knew there were secrets to successfully handling student disruptions; the trick was to find out what these secrets were. I read many books on classroom management and most of them said similar things:

"Start the year being strict and then loosen up as you go."

"The only way to really keep a class in line is to act like a witch."

"NEVER let the students see you smiling, laughing, or having fun."

And so on. It seemed that the key to teaching was to be as grumpy and disagreeable as possible to make the students fall in line. Yuck. Not the most enjoyable way to spend thirty or more years of your life. Is this really the reason why we got into teaching—to wear ourselves out being cranky every day in an attempt to intimidate kids into following directions?

This kind of authoritative approach may have succeeded with past generations but it has become outdated. In the past, young people were taught to respect adults. So when a teacher gave them a direction, the student complied and that was the end of it. But times have changed. We cannot assume that kids will automatically respect adults anymore, including their own parents. If a management plan is going to work today, it has to be reasonable and fair to students. They have to be convinced that the adult in charge is on their side, and they also have to know that the rules and consequences are in place for their benefit. If students do not believe that they are cared for, they will be much less likely to show respect.

There are times when the old style of classroom management works in the short term, but the result is still an inefficient and resentful class. This is not the best way to maximize learning. This method of teaching will eventually make coming to work torturous and will often lead to burnout.

Old School: If you want to have a well-behaved class, you must be serious, mean, and cranky to keep your students behaving well.

New School: If you want to have a well-behaved class, you must have clear rules and reasonable consequences that account for all potential disturbances.

At the end of my thirteenth year I decided to make it my mission to try to find a new and better way to handle classroom misbehavior. I am glad to say that more than twelve years after my old principal made the comments about my lack of discipline skills, I have accomplished my goal. I developed the ideas described in this book and I rarely have any stress about student behavior anymore. Classroom management no longer creates worry or concern for me. I am free to give my entire attention to other important aspects of successful teaching.

Life is too short to have to rely on being cranky and mean to get results. An effective discipline plan will not only eliminate the need for this out-of-date strategy, but it will also allow teachers to relax and be themselves so that they can get more enjoyment out of teaching! So save your "wicked witch of the west" routine for your Halloween parties. How great would it be to be able to spend all your energy on making great lessons and not have to worry about potential class disruptions? I discovered that being good at classroom management is not a skill that teachers have to be born with. It can be learned. The time has come to try something different.

1

Choosing Rules

Lawless Are They That Make Their Wills Their Law

Yeah, I've been beaten up, but I'm not beaten. I'm not beaten, and I'm not quittin'.

—from the movie *Blackboard Jungle*

The Importance of Choosing Effective Rules

As long as there have been teachers there have been classroom rules. Few would argue that a class could be run successfully without having some kind of guidelines for acceptable and unacceptable behavior. Even the most disruptive students recognize the need for these boundaries. Nobody wants chaos and disorder, at least not for the long term. If a class is to be run successfully there must be appropriate boundaries.

The most important question, of course, is not *if* teachers should have rules, but what kind of rules should be used. When teachers are choosing rules for their classes, there are two questions that are most important: (1) How many rules should be chosen? and (2) What kind of rules should there be?

Quoted from *The Two Gentlemen of Verona*.

1. How Many Rules Should Be Chosen

The appropriate number of rules that a teacher should have can vary depending on the situation. Some teachers are more comfortable than others at establishing and enforcing rules. A general guideline for a wise number of rules to have is anywhere from two to ten. Teachers who are comfortable enforcing a large number of rules can even have more than this. In his book *The Essential 55*, author and teacher Ron Clark mentions having fifty-five rules for his classes!

Contrary to popular belief, there is no magic ceiling for the number of rules that works best. Each teacher has a unique style that should not be limited by a maximum number requirement. Whatever the number of rules chosen, teachers should make that decision based on how willing they are to enforce all the rules they have selected.

Teachers can usually predict the nature of their classes before they even begin. For instance, honors classes often have different discipline issues than basic level classes. This does not necessarily mean that honors classes are better behaved than basic level ones, however. The issues between the two types are just different. If a teacher has a feeling that a certain class may not behave well, it may be wise to choose a lower number of rules.

This approach of choosing fewer rules may be the opposite of what seems logical. The reason to have fewer rules for the worst classes is that the teacher may not have the time or energy to focus on multiple misbehaviors. Only the most fundamental rules are important in this case. There is no time to get particular about rules of manners, for instance, when the teacher is just trying to keep the students from fighting. In the end, however, having too many rules is a better mistake to make than having too few. Eliminating some rules is always easier than adding them over the course of a school year.

Teachers should not be afraid to be ambitious when it comes to establishing good behavior in their classrooms. When the consequences are reasonable, there are an unlimited number of potential rules that can be chosen. As a general guideline, teachers cannot have too few or too many rules as long as they are useful.

Old School: Teachers should have a short list of rules, preferably five to ten.

New School: Teachers should have as many rules as they want, as long as they are ready to keep up with them.

TEACHER TIP
Starting the Plan in the Middle of a Term

The New Style of classroom management is designed for teachers to use from the first day of class. But what about those teachers who find out in the middle of their term that a change in classroom discipline is needed? In cases like this, teachers might want to make some adjustments when choosing their rules (consequences can generally stay the same). When starting a new classroom management plan in the middle of the term, teachers should usually choose as *few* new rules as possible.

Hopefully, some rules for the class have already been established at this point. Even if these rules have not been enforced, it would still not be wise for a teacher to add too much to the preexisting rules of the class. One or two added rules should be plenty. These new rules should be for misbehaviors that the teacher absolutely cannot allow any longer. With just a few new rules to focus on, the teacher will then have a better chance of making sure these rules are enforced.

---

2. What Kind of Rules Should Be Chosen

There are three categories of rules that successful teachers should use:

1. Rules that must exist in all successful classrooms
2. Rules for annoying behaviors that are not extreme
3. Rules that would make the classroom a paradise if followed

Rules That Must Exist in All Successful Classrooms

There are some rules that are fundamental to running a classroom successfully. For instance, students should not be able to do anything disrespectful that would disrupt the lesson or keep the teacher from teaching. Behaviors like fighting, profanity, arguing with the teacher, and so on would be in this classification. There is no place in a civilized classroom for these kinds of behaviors. Some teachers may even include excessive talking in this category.

Examples of Essential Rules

- No profanity directed at a person
- No fighting
- No physical violence or threats of violence
- No disrespecting the teacher
- No stealing

All discipline plans should include these fundamental rules, regardless of the setting. Some of these may even be in the predetermined school rules. It is a *very* bad idea to allow students to break rules that already exist for the school. Regardless of whether or not teachers agree with a school rule, they should not intentionally allow it to be broken. Teachers who intentionally violate school rules not only disrespect the administration of the school, they also risk losing credibility with students.

Rules for Annoying Behaviors That Are Not Extreme

This category of rules can have a very dramatic effect on a classroom if implemented correctly. Once the essential rules are established, a teacher can then move on to having secondary rules. These are the rules for misbehaviors that a teacher may not like but are not necessarily a huge threat to classroom security. Teachers often neglect these kinds of rules because they have to spend all of their energy enforcing the essential ones. If they are comfortable enough handling the major issues, however, the nonessential rules can really be helpful.

The nonessential rules are for misbehaviors that may seem minor compared to the others. Misbehaviors like telling someone to shut up, insulting other students, touching students, or sleeping in class would fit in this group of rules. Students who break these rules on an individual basis may not completely ruin a class, but when they happen enough times, they can still severely disrupt instruction.

Examples of Nonessential but Still Necessary Rules

- No sleeping
- No insulting other students
- No telling people to shut up
- No touching other students
- No gathering at the door before the end of the period
- No talking unless you are helping someone
- No excessive complaining
- No talking about sex, drugs, or intended violence
- No arguing/raising your voice against someone

When the consequences for breaking these nonessential rules are reasonable, teachers can confidently include them in their classroom management plans. Having a student stay for an hour of detention or calling the principal for breaking one of these rules would not make much sense. Teachers who can successfully blend the essential rules along with the nonessential ones can really begin to turn their classrooms into very positive places.

TEACHER TIP
Allowing for Different Volume Levels

Having rules for appropriate volume levels in class is always tricky. This is why it is important to be as specific as possible when setting up rules about noise level. There may be two or three different situations in class where different volume levels may be appropriate. Teachers should describe these different acceptable levels of noise in as detailed a way as possible. They can designate these levels however they want. The levels I use in class are as follows:

Dead Quiet—Being as quiet as a dead person (meaning zero noise).
Crime Level Volume—If another teacher who was not using the New Style wanted you to be quiet and you were trying to get away with talking, this is the volume level you would use.
Lunchroom Volume—Free to be as loud as you want.

Rules That Would Make the Classroom a Paradise If Followed

When teachers figure out how to master the rules in the first two categories, they can then get ambitious and consider including a third category of rules. The third rule category is for behaviors that may seem to be so wonderful that it is unreasonable to even hope they can be included. These are rules for things that are nowhere near emergencies but that would make life paradise for the teacher if they were followed. Most teachers do not even consider making these kinds of rules because they never figure out how to effectively use the other types.

The ultimate scenario for teachers would be to have little to no misbehavior at all in their classrooms. Contrary to what many teachers might think, this environment is attainable. Once the more essential rules are established, teachers can then also put the more ambitious ones into place. Examples of these kinds of rules are things such as no audible yawning, closing the door when walking in and out, or no huddling at the door before the bell rings.

Once a teacher reaches a level of competency with the more serious rules, these rules can then also be included. This level of rule making is not necessary for a teacher to have a successful classroom management plan. It is more for those who are feeling comfortable with their plans already and want to take things to a mastery level of classroom management.

Examples of "Paradise" Rules

- No audible yawning
- No leaving the door open when entering or leaving the classroom
- No getting out of your seat without permission
- No speaking without permission
- No sitting on the top of desks
- No reacting when someone else is punished
- No tattling
- No noise when passing in papers

How Rules Today Should Be Different from Those of Years Past

One of the fundamental ideas of this book is that students and classrooms are different now than they used to be. The selection of rules is no different. Since teachers in previous years have often relied on intimidation and parent phone calls to regulate their classrooms, they also required different kinds of rules. The New Style teachers who do not rely on intimidation have to make an adjustment to their rule-making process.

For whatever reasons, the existence of good manners has declined in our culture, especially among young people. As a result, teachers today would be wise to include rules that address manners. Forty or fifty years ago, teachers did not have to even consider some of the issues that exist today. The reason for discussing this occurrence here is not to assign blame on anyone for the decline of manners, but to point out that this decline does exist and that teachers must face it and deal with its impact.

In past years, teachers may not have had to deal with students who talked about sex, drugs, and violence. They may not

---

PERSONAL EXPERIENCE
Mistakes in Choosing Rules Early in My Career

Early in my career I remember asking a veteran teacher what rules he used in his classroom. His answer was something like "1. Be Respectful. 2. Be Safe. 3. Be Responsible." Eager to be successful with classroom management, I immediately copied his list of rules and used them in my classes. What I discovered, however, is that my classroom management was not effective when using them.

I am not insulting his plan or saying that it was wrong for him to use. If that was all he used, he was most likely one of the few teachers who have a natural gift for classroom management. For those lucky few who are naturals, they do not really need to be specific or detailed when it comes to choosing rules and consequences. For the majority of us, however, who do not have the natural gift for classroom management, the behavior in our classes will usually fall apart if our chosen rules are too vague.

have had students who were used to casually and frequently telling each other to shut up. The list of bad manners occurring today goes on and on. Today, poor manners are often no concern for students. In fact, they may not even realize that their manners are bad. Teachers today must often do more than just teach their subject. Lessons in manners can be just as valuable as reading, writing, and arithmetic for today's young people.

Choosing Rules That Fit a Certain Personality

One of the main points of the New Style is that it allows teachers to adjust their plans according to their own personalities. The goal is not to create some kind of cookie-cutter teacher that everyone should mold into. The best teachers are those who let their personalities show in their classrooms. Teachers who try to be someone else are asking for serious problems. Having to "fake it" too much will eventually wear a teacher out.

If teachers do not have to rely on the traditional method of intimidating students, they can be free to have any persona they want to have in the classroom. They can choose to be strict, relaxed, humorless, friendly, or whatever works best for them. Most teachers are usually some combination of all of those characteristics.

Once teachers get settled into their teaching persona, the rules they choose should be developed from their own personal character traits. Teachers who want to be strict can implement as many rules as they like and enforce them as often as they like. The ones who do not want to be as strict can still use the New Style and set their own patterns for what is acceptable. This flexibility is one of the beauties of the New Style of classroom management.

Old School: Teachers should never crack a smile for the first few weeks and then slowly get friendlier as the year progresses.

New School: Teachers should make an honest assessment of their personalities and adjust their discipline style accordingly.

The goal of the New Style is not to force every teacher into being strict and having a classroom in a perpetual state of dead quiet. The idea is to give teachers the freedom to run their classrooms *how they want them to be run*. The key is that teachers have the power! There is no rule that says teachers have to be strict to have a successful classroom. They should do what works best for them. With this New Style of classroom management, teachers decide exactly what is acceptable and what is not. These teachers can draw their own boundary lines. As long as teachers are reasonable and have good communication with students, they will generally have the freedom to act as they choose.

Key Points

- All classes need rules of some kind to be effective.
- Teachers should not be limited in the number of rules they choose. The amount of rules chosen should reflect the number of rules that they are willing to enforce.
- Rules need to fit the norms of society. Ones that may have been appropriate fifty years ago may not work today, and vice versa.
- Clarity is very important when choosing rules. Teachers should not try to implement rules that are not clear and easy to measure.
- Some rules are more essential than others. Teachers should figure out what behaviors they absolutely must have for a successful class and then build their rules from there.
- All teachers do not have to be strict and mean to be effective. The key is for teachers to figure out how strict they should be to fit their personality.

2

Choosing Consequences
The Quality of Mercy Is Not Strained

There will be no free rides, no excuses.

—from the movie *Stand and Deliver*

Choosing the Right Consequences

The choice of consequences is one of the most important parts of any successful classroom management plan. The best list of rules in the world is ineffective if appropriate consequences do not go with it. Consequences must accomplish two things to be effective: (1) They should be unpleasant enough to inspire a change of behavior and (2) They should be reasonable to students. Without these two characteristics, consequences will most likely not have their desired effect.

1. Consequences Should Be Unpleasant Enough to Inspire a Change of Behavior

The main purpose for giving a consequence is to make students think twice about breaking a rule. If students do not

---

Quoted from *The Merchant of Venice*.

believe that an action is wrong on its own merit, then they need some other motivation to prevent the behavior from happening. If students are going to consider making changes in their actions, then the bad feeling from receiving the consequence should be worse than the positive result of the misbehavior. For instance, if the punishment for robbing a bank was a sentence of ten push-ups, some people would consider committing the crime just because the risk of that punishment would be worthwhile. But if the punishment for bank robbing became a sentence of twenty years in prison, fewer people would be inclined to break the rule.

The same logic applies to the classroom. If the consequences for breaking the rules are not sufficiently unpleasant, then they will not have the desired effect of ending or reducing unwanted behavior. The joy of the misbehavior or the attention received from it will be more appealing than the risk of an unwanted consequence. This is why consequences must be unpleasant for students.

2. Consequences Should Be Reasonable to Students

Having unpleasant consequences is, of course, not the only requirement for effectiveness. There are plenty of things that are unpleasant for students that would not be appropriate consequences in a classroom. Five hours of detention for chewing gum would likely prevent the act, but it would not be an appropriate consequence. Not only is this consequence unreasonable, it would likely result in the students resenting the teacher for being unfair. Students are smart. They know when consequences are fair or not and they respond accordingly.

The Rule of Matching Severity

A simple guideline for teachers who are trying to come up with reasonable rules and consequences is the Rule of Matching Severity. This rule means that the severity of the consequence should come close to matching the severity of the misbehavior.

This rule sounds very simple, but teachers have been violating it for years. When teachers decide to handle all misbehavior with anger and intimidation, even for the smallest infractions, they are severely breaking this rule.

The Rule of Matching Severity is the reason why teachers would be wise to think about the level of seriousness of potential misbehaviors before they occur. That way, when the misbehavior happens, the teacher can be ready with a preplanned appropriate consequence. When the severity of the consequence is reasonably close to the severity of the misbehavior, the relationship between the teacher and students has not been put at risk.

This advice does not mean that teachers should have to anticipate every potential misbehavior that may occur. This may sound like an impossible task to try to accomplish, especially for newer teachers. Instead, teachers simply need to have their consequences ready for different *levels* of possible misbehaviors. A line by line matching of rules and consequences is not necessary.

Now more than ever, consequences *must* seem reasonable and fair to students to be effective. Students today have much more power and influence than those of past generations. Today, as soon as students feel they are being treated unfairly, they will often take action. They will complain to their parents, administration, the local news, and so on, and these complaints will more often than not be taken seriously.

The days are long gone when a parent would automatically take the side of the teacher in a dispute. In many cases, student misbehavior is often blamed on the teachers, the school, the long bus route, or any number of reasons. But misbehavior is *rarely* considered to be the fault of the student. Heaven forbid that that would be the case. Students now have power. How they got this power, or who is responsible for this occurrence, is not important. The important thing is that they have it at their disposal and they will use it.

As a result of these newly empowered teens, teachers have to make rules that make sense to students. Most students realize that discipline is necessary to keep order in a classroom. In fact, some of them are even desperate for order and discipline at school because they have none at home. So, in many cases, they will actually welcome a good classroom management plan. Students want to feel respected just like teachers do. A fair classroom management plan that does not simply rely on anger and intimidation from the teacher is a welcome addition for students as well as teachers.

If students do not approve of a teacher's discipline plan, they will likely make the classroom environment very unpleasant. Wise teachers will take this knowledge into consideration when developing consequences. The ones who try to run their classes like teachers of older generations, where the students had little or no voice and power, are inviting failure.

PERSONAL EXPERIENCE
Learning to Not Make Consequences Excessively Extreme

I used to think that I had to make consequences as extreme as possible to get results. For example, in my early years as a teacher, I would threaten students with a one-hour detention as a consequence for misbehavior. My thinking was that they would certainly stay in line with the threat of such extreme punishment.

I quickly learned, however, that there were some problems with this strategy. First, giving students an hour for detention was also a punishment for me. I was sentencing myself to being locked in my classroom for an hour after school. Second, I found myself letting too much misbehavior go unpunished because I did not think that it really warranted such an extreme consequence. Both of these reasons resulted in hesitation when enforcing many rules, leading to a lack of success with this method.

After many years of frustration, trying to overpunish students, I learned that to be effective, consequences only have to be severe enough to make them unpleasant, even if only slightly. Once I discovered that matching the severity of rules and consequences was the key, I was able to dramatically improve the effectiveness of my consequences.

The Old Ways of Using Consequences

In past generations, consequences were often one of three things: (1) anger and intimidation by the teacher, (2) a call home to the parent, and (3) involvement of an administrator. The problem with these consequences is that today kids are not nearly as intimidated by anger as they used to be, and parents are more likely to blame the teacher for problems than they are to blame their child. As a result, the threat of the consequences mentioned is not enough to motivate students to change their behavior. Teachers who want to be successful today can no longer try to use past methods. They are simply not as effective as they used to be.

Old School: The best consequences used by successful teachers are anger and intimidation.

New School: The best consequences are reasonable to the students and take something away that they value.

PERSONAL EXPERIENCE
Matching Consequences with Specific Misbehaviors Ahead of Time

When I first began my search for successful classroom management ideas, I sent out a survey to every teacher in my school district. I asked them how they handled specific misbehaviors. For instance, what do you do if a student talks too much in class? What do you do if a student uses profanity? My goal was to compile a list of any possible student misbehaviors and have reasonable consequences to go along with each one.

What I learned was that such a list was not needed. Most teachers did not have fifty clever consequences ready to use for every potential misbehavior. Such a list would be exhausting to try to invent and even worse to enforce. The key was not in finding specific consequences, the key was finding consequences that would match the *severity* of the misbehavior. Once I realized this important idea, my journey to finding a successful classroom management plan really began to take shape.

The Importance of Consistency with Consequences

One of the biggest challenges when dealing with consequences is the issue of consistency. Inconsistency sends the wrong messages to the students, sometimes unintentionally. When teachers give students different consequences for the same misbehavior, for instance, it would be hard to fault the student who received the more severe punishment for thinking that the teacher was being unfair. The teacher may not have this intention, but the appearance is the same nonetheless. Students who think they are not being treated fairly are much more likely to become disruptive.

Because of the tremendous importance of consistent consequences, teachers should do their best to be as clear as possible about their classroom rules and consequences. Communication between teachers and students may be the *most* important part of a successful discipline plan. Teachers should be clear from the first day and answer any questions the students may have about the discipline plan being used. This clarity can also make decision making easier for the teacher when handling discipline problems.

Furthermore, teachers must also be sure that the rules are prominently displayed in the classroom as a reminder to both them and the students. When the rules and consequences are posted and made clear, the responsibility falls on the students. Unless something happens that is beyond their control, the students have nobody to blame but themselves when they are faced with negative consequences for their actions.

Teachers should be careful to not send a message that they are intentionally trying to punish their students without cause. A spirit of cooperation and respect between teachers and students is very important. This is why teachers can no longer rely on intimidation or threats of parent phone calls to inspire good behavior. Students want to be respected, and they want to feel like they have ownership in what is taking place in the classroom. As soon as teachers try to force their will on a class, it is likely to rebel.

The Best Way to Deliver Consequences

Teachers should be careful in the way they act when delivering the consequences for misbehavior. One of the main points of the New Style of teaching is to avoid relying on a negative attitude. Therefore, teachers should do their best to be in a stoic and unemotional state when delivering consequences. Using consequences as some kind of weapon or "gotcha" will not accomplish the desired effect. Since many teachers are in the habit of using intimidation, this strategy can be a difficult adjustment. Teachers may have to remind themselves on a regular basis to keep their emotions from influencing the way they handle discipline in their classes.

This is not to say that teachers should never get angry or upset. If students do something disrespectful or dangerous, then teachers must take action, of course. The idea of the New Style is not to sit in a circle and sing "Kumbayah" every day. If students occasionally do something to warrant anger, then that is an appropriate teacher response. The point is that teachers should not overuse this tactic and handle all student misbehaviors this way.

Sometimes, teachers' moods can affect the way they handle classroom management. They can usually evaluate their emotional state before they even enter their classrooms. Students should not have to pay the price for their teachers' bad moods. Most of the time, students are not intentionally trying to bother their teachers when they misbehave, so there is rarely anything personal behind student misbehavior.

When Consequences Should Be Used

The idea that consequences should only be given for the most extreme misbehaviors is outdated. Most classroom disruption is not going to result from extreme disturbances like profanity, violence, drugs, and so on. The disruptions that cause most teachers problems are such issues as excessive talking, students arguing and insulting each other, or sleeping in class. Extreme disturbances do happen, of course. Most schools have a plan already in place to handle these extreme occurrences, however. These misbehaviors are not what the New Style is for. In most classrooms, the more minor disturbances are the ones that can destroy a potentially successful class.

TEACHER TIP
Choosing Consequences for Talking during Tests and Quizzes

Teachers often have problems devising a good way to handle talking at the end of tests and quizzes. Students who finish early often want to talk or whisper when they finish. These students are clearly not cheating; they are just restless.

The traditional consequence for talking during tests is a grade of F on the assignment. The problem created by this rule, however, is that teachers will then hesitate to give the F to students who are clearly not cheating. The result is that students talk excessively at the end of tests with the only consequence being shushes or increased anger from teachers.

The best way to handle testing situations is to designate the testing time as a "dead quiet" circumstance. This means that any word about anything will result in the first consequence in the teacher's management plan. Talking about the test, of course, will still be counted as a failing grade. This strategy gives the teachers *something* to do as a course of action if harmless whispering occurs after tests. Works like a charm!

For years, many teachers have dealt with every minor disturbance as an emergency. They would rely on the traditional method of anger and intimidation for every little mistake students made in behavior. Unfortunately, this method of classroom management can totally destroy a classroom environment. This is especially true as the students get older. In elementary school, students expect the teachers to be in complete control. Once the middle school age sets in, however, students begin to realize their ability to question and challenge the teacher's authority.

When teachers learn to use reasonable consequences, they are better able to address some of the more minor disturbances that were discussed earlier. If the primary consequences are calling the parents, giving the student an hour-long detention, or calling the administration in to help, then they will not be able to address these minor issues. If students do something like talk excessively or go to sleep in class, teachers do not have a consequence ready that is appropriate. When these mistakes are made, one of two things will likely occur: (1) the teacher will give a consequence that does not match the severity of the rule being broken, or (2) the teacher will allow the student to get away with breaking the rule.

In either case, the atmosphere of the class and the relationship between the teacher and students will likely crumble.

The actual consequences chosen by teachers are not that important. Teachers can create their own consequences to fit their environment best. The key for teachers is to find a group of less severe, but still effective, consequences to include as the cornerstone of their discipline plans. When these are added along with the standard school consequences for extreme misbehaviors, teachers can then discover that they have the power to have wonderfully behaved classes and great relationships with their students.

TEACHER TIP
Using the Dead Quiet Consequence for Individuals and Classes

One of my favorite consequences to employ is the use of the dead quiet period. This strategy is a great application of the New Style of classroom management. When used with individuals, a dead quiet period of either three or five minutes is given on the first warning. If students break a class rule, they then have to be totally quiet (like a dead person) for the given time. This is not a severe punishment by any means, but it is uncomfortable enough to deter misbehavior from students. Also, it gives the teacher a break from the student's aggravating behavior and noise. If the student talks during the dead quiet time, they would then move up the teacher's list of consequences.

The dead quiet period can also be given to the class as a whole. If there are too many students breaking a rule at once, such as excessive talking, then a blanket dead quiet penalty can be given to the entire group. My rule for this situation is that any student who talks during this time then moves up the list of consequences.

The dead quiet period is also the only consequence that I give to an entire group. In the interest of fairness, I never give the entire class a longer group detention or another mass consequence. The only exception may be to keep the entire class an extra minute or thirty seconds for a group violation of a rule.

The Lessons Students Learn from Consequences

One of the most important nonacademic lessons teachers can teach is that actions have consequences. If people break the speed limit too many times, they will get fined and eventually lose their right to drive. If employees regularly show up to work late, they will be fired. These are the kinds of lessons that students can and should be learning in school, rather than having to learn them the hard way when they are on their own.

Unfortunately, the lessons of consequences are being taught less and less in schools today. Often, the adults in charge would rather protect children from every possible unpleasant thing that may happen to them. As a result, scores in Little League games are no longer kept, schools do away with giving failing grades in some places, and students are coddled all the way up to high school.

While the intentions of the adults in charge who make these kinds of decisions may be good, the result is the crippling of the children involved. Protecting students from negative consequences will keep them from learning how to deal with difficult situations in life. Negative events happen to everyone; everything is not going to go perfectly all the time. Well-meaning parents, teachers, and administrators will not always be there to shelter kids from the pain of failure or defeat.

Education is about more than just reading, writing, and arithmetic. It is also about preparing students for life. The more teachers can prepare students to deal with adversity, the better off these students will be when they are on their own. School is a great setting for students to learn these lessons, whether it be in the classroom or during an extracurricular activity. Instead of protecting students from every possible negative outcome, educators should be allowing students the chance to face negative consequences for their actions. When this occurs, the students will learn coping skills for dealing with the negative, and their education will not have partially failed them.

Key Points

- Selecting appropriate consequences is essential to having a successful classroom management system.
- Consequences do not need to be extreme. They only need to be unpleasant enough to result in a change in behavior.

- In the New Style of classroom management, consequences must be reasonable to students. If consequences do not make sense to students, there is much less of a chance that they will be effective.
- The Rule of Matching Severity states that the severity of consequences must match the severity of the rules broken. This rule is the key to having a classroom management plan make sense to students.
- The old consequences used by teachers such as calling parents, getting angry, and removing students from class are often no longer valid. The New Style of classroom management is much more effective.
- The best way to implement consequences is to have a stoic and unemotional attitude. Teachers should let their plans be sufficient enough to send the intended message. They do not need any negative attitude to help the situation.
- Students need to learn that there are consequences for their actions, both positive and negative. Schools who try to protect their students from the unpleasantness of facing consequences are only crippling them for future difficult events they will face in life.

3

Outline of the New Style of Classroom Management

I Must Be Cruel, Only to Be Kind (Unless I Have a Plan)

> Discipline should not be the enemy of enthusiasm!
>
> —from the movie *Lean on Me*

There is a very real teacher emergency taking place. Our educational system is in a state of decline. Many educators today have great teaching skills in their subject areas but do not have minimum skills needed for successful classroom management. There is also a large number of people who are not teaching at all, those who have left the profession or have not even entered it because of a fear of bad student behavior. As a result of these two situations, the quality of education our children are getting is not nearly as good as it could be. A New Style of teaching is needed to save our teachers, our schools, and the education of our children.

The Dream

Imagine a classroom that has very little disruption or student misbehavior. The teacher is relaxed and clearly in control.

Paraphrased from *Hamlet*.

Talking, excessive noise, and other possible disruptions occur only if they are permitted. The teacher has great enthusiasm for the material being taught, and the students respond with energetic participation. This environment may sound too good to be true. For many teachers, this scenario is a fairy tale, a seemingly impossible dream.

Believe it or not, though, this classroom environment is attainable. And it is possible to achieve regardless of the age, class size, or academic level of the students. Though the classroom described may not be very common in schools today (yet), it does exist. The number of classes like this is growing, including ones that follow the plans outlined in this book.

The old methods of classroom management have lost their effectiveness for a number of reasons. Once it became obvious that the "old school" methods were limited, the first logical step was to develop a New Style of classroom management. An essential part of this new plan would be to find one that would work in all classrooms from middle schools to colleges.

Obstacles to the Dream

One of the biggest problems with classroom management is that there are usually only three choices for teachers when handling misbehaviors:

1. Remove the student from the classroom.
2. Be mean, yell, or scream until the student is intimidated into behaving.
3. Call home.

The problem with these choices is that there are many times when they are inappropriate, unsuccessful, unreasonable, or all of the above.

1. Removing Students from the Classroom

All teachers must accept the fact that removing a student from class is sometimes the only reasonable answer to certain misbehaviors. There is a point where students misbehave so severely that it is impractical and, at times, dangerous to allow them to stay. The problem comes when teachers try to *overuse* this method as if it were the only choice possible. On the contrary, students should only be removed in extreme situations.

There are only a few scenarios that warrant removing students from class. For instance, students who are a danger to others or who have been extremely disrespectful to the teacher fit into this category. Outside of these kinds of circumstances, however, this method is usually not appropriate. This dilemma often results in one of the biggest discipline mistakes made by teachers today: *mismatching the severity of consequences and misbehaviors.* In most schools, the kinds of misbehaviors that warrant removal rarely happen (with some exceptions, of course), which means this method should rarely be used. *Estimated percentage of appropriate use: 1–5 percent.*

2. Being Mean, Yelling, or Screaming until Intimidating the Student into Behaving

Ah yes, the classic teaching method used for controlling misbehavior. The advice to "just be mean at first and then slowly ease up as you go" has been used for so long that just about every teacher has heard it. Like the method of removing a student, this strategy also sometimes has a place in teaching. Some teachers may disagree with this point, but there are times when it is appropriate for a teacher to get angry with a student.

Much like the first method, however, the kinds of situations that require this reaction are hopefully not the norm. The potential problem for teachers, once again, is overuse of the tactic. There are many teachers who use this approach for nearly *every* discipline issue that comes up in class. Every little thing that goes wrong is handled with anger. Teachers often quickly fall into the frustrating pattern of saying "Stop it . . . Stop it . . . Stop it . . . Stop it!" until finally losing their temper and becoming completely frustrated with the student. Talk about the makings for a long day!

This strategy is a big mistake for a number of reasons. First, even if this method works, it often leads to an adversarial relationship between the teacher and students. The class may be coerced into silence, but the result is an extremely negative atmosphere. If students are in a constant state of fear and worry, they can rarely learn to their potential. Also, if teachers have to be mean and angry all of the time, then they will usually end up resenting both their jobs and their students.

Teaching is supposed to be a rewarding job; there should be a feeling of accomplishment at the end of each day. If teachers have to resort to using anger on a regular basis, then it will be hard for them to feel good about what they are doing. The effects will be even worse if it is not their personality to be strict. If teachers have to put on too much of an act to run their classes, they will become worn out. Teachers who insist on using this method of discipline will likely end up exhausted, cranky, burned out, and counting every minute until the end of the day, the weekend, and summer vacation. *Estimated percentage of appropriate use: 2–5 percent.*

PERSONAL EXPERIENCE
Using Anger and Intimidation as a Discipline Method

I actually tried the anger and intimidation approach to discipline early in my teaching career, choosing to be serious and cranky at all times. Yes, my classes were fairly well-behaved, but by the end of the day I was in a terrible mood. I was coaching at the time, and I was often in no mood to go to practice after school. Also, I had no interest in going to school sporting events or other extracurricular activities, or anywhere else where I might see students. I had created an antagonistic "teacher against student" atmosphere, and it resulted in a predictably negative relationship between my students and me. It soon became clear that if I would have kept up this approach I would have burned out and left teaching years ago.

---

3. Call Home

There may be some disagreement from teachers with this concept. Many principals stress the importance of making parent phone calls. The idea is that if teachers call parents about a student who is misbehaving, then the parent will correct the child's behavior. Not so fast. Most teachers would agree that this strategy rarely works! This is not to say that home phone calls *never* work for anyone. Some teachers love this method of behavior management and still use it with varying success. But as times change, relying on parent correction of student behavior seems to be working less and less.

In past generations, a parent phone call would mean trouble for the child at home, and students feared the consequences. These days, however, the fear of punishment from parents has diminished. As a result, a parent phone call often has little effect on a student's behavior. In today's culture, the norm seems to be for young people to question authority; they no longer automatically respect adults.

The result of this change for teachers is that discipline now has to make sense to students to be effective. They are no longer going to do what they are told just because a teacher said so *or* just because their parents said so. If teachers' classroom management plans are not reasonable to students, then they will fight both the teacher and the plan for the duration of the term.

Contrary to popular belief, parents should be called only to be *notified* about what is happening with their child but not as a strategy to fix poor classroom conduct. Unfortunately, just about every book written about classroom management suggests using the parent call as a consequence, as if the call will change the student's behavior. This strategy is outdated!

The days when the parent call could be counted on as a deterrent to misbehavior are over. Many times, even the parents have problems with their kids at home. So teachers should go ahead and call a parent if there is something that they should hear about: a bad grade, inappropriate behavior, and so on. But holding out hope that parent calls will improve the way the child acts in class is foolish. *Estimated percentage of appropriate use: 5–10 percent.*

Old School: Every good discipline plan uses the parent call as a possible consequence.

New School: Parent calls should be used for notifying parents and giving them information *only*. It is unrealistic to count on a call to a parent to improve a child's conduct in class.

Notice the percentages at the end of each discussion about the appropriate use of the "traditional methods" for classroom management. The total for all three comes to about 20 percent. That leaves an estimated 80 percent of classroom misbehavior remaining that would not appropriately apply to the traditional methods of classroom management!

When teachers do not have any recourse for dealing with this remaining 80 percent of student misbehaviors, they end up either letting them go unaddressed or they misapply traditional methods. These things cause stress for both teachers and students and result in an unproductive classroom environment. This discrepancy is one of the inspirations for writing this book. There is way too much misbehavior taking place in classrooms that could be handled in a better way.

The Answer to the Problem

This book describes a simple but effective plan for handling those situations that are not extreme but are still disruptive to learning. The key to this plan is that it provides fast, easy to use, and reasonable consequences for these kinds of misbehaviors. This New Style of classroom management allows for the teacher to always be in control of the classroom!

Before Setting Up a Classroom Management Plan, Some Important Decisions Should Be Made

1. Which student misbehaviors are nonnegotiable, that is, what behaviors should be completely eliminated in the classroom?
2. Which misbehaviors are annoying and would be nice to eliminate but are not essential to a smoothly run classroom?
3. Just how much talking should be allowed before enforcing a consequence?

Teachers in difficult situations such as having an unruly class would be wise to deal only with the nonnegotiable behaviors when setting up their plan. An ambitious teacher may want to add the secondary rules later after everything is running smoothly.

Once answers for these questions have been developed, the time has come to implement the plan. A list of one to ten misbehaviors should be chosen that should be eliminated from class. This list should be considered very carefully. Once this has been decided, a poster listing the rules and consequences should be displayed in the classroom. This poster will serve as a constant reminder to both the students and teacher about the details of the plan.

Clarity and communication are the most important parts of a successful discipline plan. The students must know exactly what is expected from them and exactly what will happen to them if they do not comply. The importance of this communication should not be overlooked!

TEACHER TIP
Starting the Plan in the Middle of a Term

If you do not have the luxury of starting a plan with your class from day one, you would be wise to narrow down your list of potential offenses, at least at first. Anywhere from two to five rules would be best in this situation. If you give them much more than that, then they will have a difficult adjustment. In this situation I would recommend focusing on nonnegotiable offenses only.

What Is a Classroom Management Plan?

A classroom management plan is a list of rules and consequences that will be given if those rules are not followed. These rules and consequences are usually posted somewhere in the classroom and are often sent home to the students' parents. Most teachers have some form or other of a classroom management plan. The effectiveness of these plans is what is in question.

The New Style Plan!

The following steps will be taken for all students who break any of the rules that have been established in a standard New Style classroom management plan.

Step 1: Warning (5 Minute Magic)

Student will immediately be given a period of five minutes in which they cannot say a word (called "dead quiet"). During this time, any talking will result in the student having to move up to the next step on the consequences list. This procedure can be used with individuals or with the class as a whole. If this consequence is given to the entire class, only individuals can be additionally punished for extra talking.

Consequences are never given to the class as a whole with the exception of the five-minute warning penalty. The goal is to keep students from being unfairly punished. Since all of the consequences after the initial warning result in after-class detention, too many students would be unfairly punished if this consequence was given to the class as a whole.

This first step is the key to the plan, and is called "5 Minute Magic." There are a few reasons why this step is so important. First, students are given consequences with the first step. There is no room for students to have a "buffer" where they know that they can misbehave until after a warning is given. This buffer zone is a major weakness of traditional behavior plans. With 5 Minute Magic, students have an immediate consequence the first time a rule is broken.

The second reason the five-minute warning consequence is so important is that students are immediately required to be quiet. The most common misbehavior among students is too much talking, and this automatic quiet time can be a much needed break for the teacher. Even though the time period is short, students will often remain reasonably quiet even after the penalty has been served. And of course, the point has been made with no yelling or anger from the teacher. This step can be like magic because it can result in a misbehaving student or class becoming perfectly quiet in an instant. When used correctly, this method almost seems like the teacher has spread some magic, quiet-inducing dust over the student or the entire class.

Step 2: One-Minute Detention after Class

This consequence is to be given at the end of the class period in which it was assigned, with no exceptions. Students are required to sit and be quiet for the entire minute. If students are worried about being late to their next class, then they should be told to avoid detention in the first place! This explanation places the responsibility on the students and gives them control of the outcome. That way students cannot complain that they were tricked or "made" to do anything.

Step 3: Fifteen Minutes of Detention

This consequence must be served before or after school, either on the same day as the misbehavior or on the following school day. Students may sometimes be given some flexibility on this one, however. Activities are sometimes scheduled in advance, so teachers should be reasonable and let students reschedule a detention up to a week later under special circumstances. If there is not a great reason to reschedule, however, the detention should be served quickly. Students should not be told about this exception ahead of time! There should still be room for fairness and understanding. The goal, of course, is to have an environment of cooperation, not one of teacher against student.

Step 4: Removal from Class

This consequence can be accomplished with an in-school suspension (ISS) or call to administrator for removal (or whatever is called for in the school policy). It can also be given for an unexcused absence from detention.

> **TEACHER TIP**
> **Avoid Showing Anger**
>
> Teachers should make sure to not show anger when implementing the plan for less extreme misbehaviors. The idea is that the teacher is on the same side as the students, not against them. The best demeanor for a teacher when giving a consequence is to be stoic and unemotional. Teachers can sometimes even get away with giving the consequences with a smile! Just be careful to not fall back into the old way of handling discipline with incrementally growing doses of anger.

One of the most useful phrases teachers can use is "Be careful!" This phrase can be very useful when students are getting close to breaking a rule. The rules and consequences of a plan can be treated like they have a life of their own, not even connected to the teacher. The teacher and students are in the fight together to help them avoid punishment! If teachers can act convincingly like they and the students are working together in the same fight against the plan, then they have won.

Why Such a Simple Plan Works

1. Young People *Hate* Losing Their Freedom

Even if a penalty is as short as five quiet minutes or even one minute, young people hate giving up their free time. So the penalty is uncomfortable for them, even in such small doses. This small amount of discomfort is all that is needed to make them want to change their behavior.

2. The Penalties Are Reasonable

Rules and consequences must make sense and be reasonable to the students if any behavior plan is going to work. If rules are not reasonable, students will fight them.

3. The Plan Is Easy to Use

Once teachers get used to it, they can use the New Style plan without slowing down when teaching. Either the teacher is signing the book quickly or the students are getting up and signing it with limited interruption. If students do choose to interrupt, then they will be moved up to the next step in the list of consequences. Teachers must be sure not to forget when students are serving a five-minute penalty so that they are ready to enforce the next consequence if the students slip up and talk. Consistency is very important.

4. Easy and Organized Record Keeping

Since the names are being written down, teachers have an instant record of who was penalized, when it happened, and how often. Punishments can now be easily given for misbehaviors that are repeated over days or months. The students are accountable and they know it.

Also, it is important that students' names are recorded each time they receive a consequence. This can be done either by the teacher or the students themselves (to be decided by the teacher from the beginning). To save time, a checkmark can be added for each stage after the warning so that the student's name does not have to be written out multiple times on a given day. Another time-saving option may be to write only the student's first name and last initial. The record keeping should be smooth enough that instruction can continue without interruption. The name book should be easily accessible and in the open so that it can be signed quickly.

Also, if the choice is made for students to sign, there should be a corresponding rule that students cannot cause any disturbance when someone is signing. There is no need for a lot of commotion or attention when someone is being punished. Students will also often try to act like they do not care about getting punished. Teachers should not be fooled by this tactic. They care.

TEACHER TIP
Making Detention Rules

Teachers have various options for conducting detention. They may range from making students sit and do absolutely nothing to letting them do what they want as long as they stay in the room. The specifics are not important. Detention rules should probably fall somewhere in the middle of those extremes. Some teachers have even forbidden schoolwork being done during detention. All of this is up to the teacher to decide. And remember, the longest suggested detention time for less extreme misbehaviors is only fifteen minutes.

Potential Misbehaviors That Can Be Handled Using the Plan (Teacher's Option)

- Excessive talking.
- Telling someone to shut up.
- Profanity—casual. (This includes things like swearing to yourself when you get a bad grade, inadvertent profanity, etc. This is profanity not directed toward another person.)
- Getting out of your seat without permission.
- Insulting someone.
- Talking about sex, drugs, or intended violence.
- Putting your hands on someone.
- Forgetting materials (pencil, paper, calculator, etc.).
- Gathering at the door before the bell rings at the end of the period.
- Excessive complaining.
- General incivility (basically anything the teacher decides is uncivilized).
- Making any noise or commotion while signing the detention book or signing the book in a silly way (large letters, etc.).

Sample Plan

Rules

1. No talking when the teacher is talking
2. No insults
3. No telling someone to shut up
4. No getting out of your seat without permission
5. No putting your hands on someone

Consequences

1. Five minutes of dead quiet
2. One minute of detention (after class)
3. Fifteen minutes of detention (that day or the next day)
4. Removal from class (ISS or call to administrator)

Key Points

- There is an emergency in teaching. A change in methods used for classroom management is needed.
- The old methods of classroom management are no longer effective. Calling home, being mean, and removing students from class are rarely useful anymore.
- Most teachers today do not have any reasonable plan for dealing with about 80 percent of potential misbehaviors.
- Teachers should be as organized as possible when installing a classroom management plan. They are much better off being proactive rather than reactive.
- The defining characteristics of the New Style plan for classroom management are that it is simple, clearly organized, and easy to implement. It has fair and reasonable rules and consequences that fit teachers' personalities.
- The New Style plan works because it is reasonable to students but also uses consequences that are uncomfortable enough to deter undesirable behavior.

4

Potential Problems with the New Style of Classroom Management

Modest Doubt Is Called the Beacon of the Wise

> I stand upon my desk to remind myself that we must constantly look at things in a different way.
>
> —from the movie *Dead Poets Society*

The central theme of this book is that there should be a new approach to classroom management and to teaching in general. Whenever such a change is going to take place, there are potential problems that may arise as a result. Teachers, therefore, need to guard against these potential bumps in the road. They should be proactive in their approach to changing the way they handle classroom management. If teachers can see the potential problems ahead of time, they can make the issues much easier to handle when they do happen.

Potential Problems with the New Style

1. Difficulties for Veteran Teachers

Sometimes old habits are hard to break. Many teachers are so used to relying on a negative attitude and intimidation as the

---

Quoted from *Troilus and Cressida*.

main tools of their classroom management style that they have a difficult time making changes. If these teachers want to successfully adjust their methods, however, they need to make up their minds and commit. Once they realize how effective and low stress the New Style can be, these teachers will most likely be more than willing to make the effort.

2. Difficulties for New Teachers

New teachers have both advantages and disadvantages when it comes to learning the New Style of management. It is true that new teachers do not have the baggage of ingrained habits that veteran teachers have. They do have their own separate issues, however.

Many first and second year teachers are still trying to figure out their teaching identities. All teachers must develop their own teaching personalities. Do they want to be strict, fun, mean, friendly, or something entirely different? Do they want to give a lot of homework? How will they weigh tests? When new teachers begin their careers, they are often thrown into the fire, so to speak, so they have to come up with answers to these questions quickly.

Often with little time to prepare once they get their first job and with little training in classroom management, new teachers are quickly forced to invent their teaching identities. As a result, many of them simply copy the style of a favorite teacher that they may have had, at least at first. While this strategy may be fine for short-term survival, it is not a good long-term plan.

No teacher will be a totally blank slate when it comes to developing an individual classroom management style. Everyone has influences from their past in some form or another. The problem comes when teachers get hung up on those past influences and cannot get away from them. When new teachers learn to let go of the idea of trying to be like someone else, they can really begin to open the door to a much more satisfying teaching experience.

Another reason for not trying to copy old teachers is that the style they used may have only worked with their particular group of students. Sometimes teachers have different personalities from class to class. This is usually a direct response to the variety of personalities involved. The way that a teacher taught in one particular class may not even represent their usual teaching method.

Very few teachers have the exact same personality in every class. And since most teachers will be teaching a variety of ability levels, just relying on styles that were used in their classes growing up will not always work now that they are teaching their own classes. Chances are that students who become teachers took college prep classes. Therefore, they most likely did not have a chance to see their teachers deal with many behavior challenges.

Trying to act like someone else is never a good idea in any profession, but it is especially true in teaching. Someone who is usually laid back and friendly should not try to force themselves to be strict and mean in the classroom because someone told them that is how it should be done. This kind of acting puts

---

PERSONAL EXPERIENCE
Trying to Be Like a Former Teacher

Most teachers first start out trying to be like a teacher from their past. When I was in high school, I had a tremendous math teacher (who also happened to be my basketball coach). He was very relaxed and funny, but when it was time to be serious he was all business. He seemed like the greatest teacher in the world to me. I have a similar personality to his, so when I first started teaching I decided to try to copy him. My classes went well for the most part, but when students started to get too talkative I did not really have an answer. Getting angry with them would not work because I had already established my friendly personality. I could not just get friendlier with them because they would not respond to that method either.

I realized that I had only copied the *good* things that I remembered about my old teacher. Since the math classes that I took were mostly upper level ones, I rarely got to see how he handled many discipline issues. I then remembered something that I had completely forgotten about.

In those days, students were allowed to be teachers' assistants. We would grade papers, take roll, and so forth. I was allowed to be the teacher's assistant for my math teacher's seventh grade pre-algebra class. The class was so talkative and out of control; he seemed to always be stressed out. He did not seem to know what to do with them. When I remembered that situation, I realized that the laid-back, nice guy persona will eventually not work if classes misbehave enough. There is nothing wrong with being friendly and nice, just be sure to be ready with an organized way to handle behavior problems.

too much stress on teachers and will almost certainly lead to burnout. The only exception to acting like someone else is when it comes to showing confidence. Faking confidence may be a necessity for survival, especially early on.

3. Giving Up on a Plan Too Early

Sometimes there is a temptation to give up on a discipline plan early if something new is not working. When using the New Style of classroom management, there is a chance that it may not immediately be successful. Sometimes both students and teachers need time to adjust. Just because the class does not become immediately perfectly behaved does not mean that the teacher's plans will not work. Once students realize that the teacher is consistent and committed to his or her plan, they will usually start to fall in line.

4. Establishing Too Many Rules

There is no set limit to the number of rules needed to run a classroom management plan successfully. However, teachers should be careful not to make more rules than they can keep track of consistently. Rules should only be chosen that can be easily handled by the teacher. The teacher loses credibility with a class when rules are established but not enforced.

5. Using Unclear Rules

One important aspect of rules chosen by teachers is that these rules must be as clear as possible. If they are clear to both the teacher and student, they are much easier to enforce. Unclear rules lead to miscommunication between the teacher, student, and parents. For instance, vague rules like "be respectful" or "behave well" are not specific enough to effectively enforce. Unclear rules will likely cause stress and frustration for everyone involved.

6. Giving Consequences with an Attitude

A key element of the New Style is that teachers must not use anger or negative emotions as a tool to enforce their rules.

Teachers must go out of their way to keep their mood as stoic and unemotional as possible. The New Style of classroom management demands that anger not be a primary discipline strategy for teachers.

7. Not Displaying the Rules and Consequences Prominently

A clear display of the rules helps both the teacher and students to remember how teachers' management plans are organized. This display should be in a prominent place in the classroom and large enough for everyone to see clearly.

8. Not Sending the Plan Home to Parents Early

Parents must be alerted when teachers intend to begin using the New Style of classroom management. Teachers who make an early attempt to be on good terms with parents will be glad in the long run. A description of the management plan should be sent home on the first day of school along with a requirement for a parent and student signature.

9. Adding Too Many Rules after the Term Has Begun

Even though adding a rule or two after the term begins is not completely out of the question, making these kinds of changes is not recommended. Teachers need to put some time and effort into establishing a management plan that they are comfortable with from the beginning. Too many changes make teachers seem indecisive.

10. Letting Students Argue or React When Receiving a Consequence

Students should not be able to complain when receiving a consequence. If the rules and consequences have been made clear, there is nothing for students to argue about. There is nothing wrong with even including a rule about excessive complaining.

11. Whining When Giving Consequences to Students

This practice is not only unprofessional but it also appeals to the emotion of the students. Consequences given with little emotion are almost always the best choice, of course. Using little emotion keeps the situation from becoming personal and out of control.

12. Letting Substitute Teachers Allow Misbehavior

Teachers should make an effort to ensure their management plan is consistent for substitute teachers even when they are away from school. Detailed explanations of management plans should be left for the substitute teachers. Students should also be warned ahead of time about the consequences for misbehaving for a sub.

13. Not Having a Consequence Connected to the First Warning

When students know that they will not be punished for their initial misbehaviors, they often act as if they have a "free pass" with a warning. A small consequence with the first warning eliminates this "buffer" mentality.

Old School: Veteran teachers are set in their ways and resist making any drastic changes to their styles of discipline.

New School: Veteran teachers can change their style of classroom management as long as they guard themselves against falling back into their old ways.

TEACHER TIP
Be Committed to Whatever Plan You Choose to Implement!

Whatever classroom management plan you choose to implement, you must make an effort to stay committed to it! If a plan looks like it is not working at first do not give up on it quickly. Sometimes the students have to see that teachers are sincere and committed when they say that they will enforce a particular plan. Students may complain, they may earn a lot of consequences early on, or they may even say that your plan does not work. Teachers must be careful to not let students talk them out of doing what they planned. There is nothing wrong with making small adjustments here and there, but scrapping a plan too early makes a teacher look weak. Do not give up too soon!

Key Points

- Teachers who try a different style of classroom management may run into problems from various sources.
- Veteran teachers may have to constantly remind themselves to handle their classroom management differently if they are making drastic changes.
- Newer teachers have to overcome trying to copy previous teachers from their own experiences as students.
- Choices for rules and consequences should be made according to what fits teachers' needs and goals for their classes. There is more than one way to implement the New Style.
- Many problems that teachers have with student misbehavior are the result of poor communication.
- There should be some kind of consequence given for the first warning to keep students from having a buffer for misbehavior before any punishment occurs.

5

The Mind-set Needed to Teach Successfully

Keeping Stress Low

There Is Nothing Either Good or Bad, but Thinking Makes It So

> According to most studies, people's number one fear is public speaking. Number two is death. Death is number two. Does that sound right? This means to the average person, if you go to a funeral, you're better off in the casket than doing the eulogy.
>
> —Jerry Seinfeld

No matter how great a teacher's discipline plan is, there is no getting around the fact that the job will be stressful. When teachers are in a class full of students, it is as if they are on stage performing. Some of the performance will be planned, but much of it will have to be thought of in the moment. Even for people who are used to speaking in public, the fear and discomfort that comes from public speaking never disappears completely.

One of the main causes of stress for teachers is having to be in a constant state of awareness of the actions of their students. They cannot let students get away with too much misbehavior. This duty is not something that most people who work in a

---

Quoted from *Hamlet*.

nine-to-five job have to deal with. The constant demand for attention and awareness can be a huge cause of stress for teachers.

There is no way to completely eliminate pressures of the job, of course. Wise teachers, though, look for ways to lower stress in any way possible. The good news is that there are many things that teachers can do to help lower the stress that comes from teaching.

Strategies for Reducing Stress for Teachers

1. Exercise

Like people in other occupations, teachers should be careful to take care of themselves. Getting enough exercise is good for both general health and attitude. Teachers should avoid getting into a habit of sitting around all day grading and planning without ever exercising. The temptation to go home and lounge around eating ice cream and watching television as a regular way to deal with stress should be avoided.

2. Get Enough Sleep

This may be the most important method of stress reduction for teachers. So many teachers procrastinate and end up staying up way too late working. Not only is this bad for physical health, lack of sleep can also have adverse effects on mental health and stress levels. Studies vary as to how much sleep is considered enough, but a minimum of six hours with a goal of seven to eight hours is wise. Of course, things happen occasionally that demand a late night and just cannot be avoided. Teachers would be doing themselves a big favor, however, if they got an appropriate amount of sleep on a regular basis.

3. Eat Right

This one falls into a similar category as getting exercise. Eating right is another part of staying healthy, maximizing energy, and so on. Eating healthy foods can also serve to reduce levels of stress. Contrary to popular belief, healthy eating does not include regular caffeine consumption, so excessive amounts of coffee and soda should be avoided!

4. Have a Social/Separate Life Away from School

This one is very important, especially for teachers who are single. Teachers must do whatever they can to avoid burnout, and making teaching their life is an easy way to do this. Teachers should be dedicated to being great, of course, but the job should not consume them. Sometimes teachers have to force themselves to get out and socialize, even if they do not feel like it. If having an active social life is not made a priority, teachers may too easily fall into the trap of letting their teaching career become consuming.

PERSONAL EXPERIENCE
Having a Separate Life Away from Teaching

I have always been careful to have a separate life away from teaching. Even for those teachers who love every minute of the job, there can still be dangerous consequences for getting too consumed with it.

I have always tried to live at least twenty miles away from the school where I teach. This helps me avoid having to see people associated with the school every time I go to the grocery store or the movies. Nobody likes an impromptu parent/teacher conference in the frozen foods section. Also, I try my best to do as much work as possible at school. If all a teacher does is go to school and teach, go home and do schoolwork, and then go to bed, they are going to eventually wear out. Making sure that teaching does not become the entire focus of my life is one of the main ways I have been able to avoid burning out from teaching.

---

5. Do Not Teach or Tutor during the Summer

Administrators may not like to hear this discussion but this book is about helping teachers so they can get over it. Teaching summer school and tutoring may both sound like great ideas at first. The truth is that most teachers would benefit from taking time away from anything *close* to teaching. If extra money is needed, there are plenty of other part-time jobs available during the summer. Even if the pay may not be quite as good as teaching or tutoring, a summer job that is not related to teaching can help teachers get refreshed for the next school year. Also, doing education-related work during the summer and holidays can easily contribute to burnout when there is no break from the education world.

6. Make an Effort to Get Along with Coworkers

There will always be people in any work environment that do not get along. This is just a result of human nature. However, teachers can make an effort to minimize potential conflict with coworkers if they make a point to handle things themselves and not rush into confrontations.

Of course, the best advice for avoiding conflict can simply be not to spend time around people that clearly invite conflict. Since most of the time during the school day is spent in the classroom anyway, avoiding teachers who are not agreeable is usually not all that difficult.

7. Do as Much Work at School as Possible

Sometimes this goal is not realistic for teachers, but it can be very helpful if possible. Teachers with children at home, or who have other commitments, can often not afford to spend time at school after hours. However, for those who can do so, this strategy can save a lot of stress. Getting work done at school helps teachers have a separate life at home. There is something very comforting about being able to leave school with nothing hanging over until the next day. Accomplishing this goal takes planning and dedication but it is well worth the effort.

8. Have an Efficient Grading System

Efficiency in grading is extremely important. Sometimes an efficient grading system can take a little while to develop. Newer teachers would be wise to get input from veteran teachers about what works best for them. Efficiency is the key! Grading every minute detail is not necessarily always important.

The subject and age of students being taught greatly impact the best grading system, of course. Teachers should prioritize what parts of the overall grade are most important. For teachers of high school age and above, test grades should usually have the highest impact. Teachers should not waste time overemphasizing grades on smaller, nontest assignments.

9. Do Not Talk about Problem Classes or Students at Lunch

This idea is not only a matter of relieving stress, but also an issue of manners. Lunchtime at schools is too often used as a griping session for teachers. Believe it or not, most other teachers do not want to hear about the problems of their coworkers! Complaining brings a negative atmosphere and adds to everyone's stress level. Also, it is not fair to students to have their names mentioned in a negative way publicly.

10. Get to School on Time (or Even a Little Early)

Being late to work may not be an emergency, but it can have an effect on overall stress. Arriving even five minutes earlier than usual can save a lot of stress and aggravation. This punctuality can also give teachers extra time to get prepared, and it never hurts to look good to the administration. Little things like punctuality add up when it comes to stress. Wise teachers look for ways to reduce these problems during their day.

11. Do Not Rely on Anger and Intimidation as Your Primary Discipline Method

This topic has already been discussed in depth in this book. Not only is the method ineffective, but relying on anger and intimidation for discipline can be a major cause of stress as well. Life is too short to have to live like this.

12. Be Careful about Overextending Yourself

Teachers sometimes fall into the trap of not being able to say no. Many times, extracurricular supervision comes with the job, so there can be some obligation for it. However, teachers should be careful about saying yes to everything that is offered to them. Overextending can easily lead to burnout, even if the activities are enjoyable. If the opportunity is there to say no, teachers should not feel bad about opting out. If possible, it is best to do only one or two extracurricular activities at most.

13. Do Not Worry about Popularity

Teachers who are worried about being friends with students are inviting trouble. Concern about reputation with the students can lead to compromise and therefore unneeded stress. Teachers can still be friendly without having to compromise for popularity.

14. Plan Each Day as If You Were Going to Be Observed

Some administrators may visit classrooms more often than others but all teachers should plan each day as if they were being observed. First of all, teachers owe their best effort to the students. Second, this strategy reduces the fear that an administrator might walk in and catch something that should not be taking place. Having well-planned lessons is a great way to reduce stress.

15. Focus on Serving Students, Not Yourself

Most teachers may not think of the profession this way, but the job is service oriented. Teachers are not hired to just try to survive each day and each school year with as little difficulty as possible. They are hired to serve students. Sometimes teachers lose this perspective. If a teacher is not involved in the career to serve students, then they may want to consider doing something else.

16. Do Not Let Students Tell You That Your Discipline Plan Does Not Work

Some students can be very sneaky. They will do whatever they can to try to weaken a teacher's authority. Teachers who want to teach using the New Style should disregard comments by students about the plan not working and stick to it!

17. Do Not Use Emotion When Administering Discipline

Even teachers using the New Style of discipline are at risk of falling into this trap. Classroom management is difficult enough without adding the stress of using anger. Teachers are human, so they will still be tempted to lose control or get agitated when things do not go well. If this happens, the best thing to do is just try to learn from mistakes and avoid repeating them in the future. The goal is to be as unemotional and stoic as possible when giving consequences.

18. Act Confident and In Control—Even If This Is Not True

This is one of the keys for successful teaching. Acting confident and in control long enough will eventually make it true. Teachers should act quickly and decisively and never show fear.

TEACHER TIP
Coming to School in a Bad Mood

There are some days that we just wake up in a bad mood. Sometimes there may be a reason for it, other times there may not be. When this happens, however, it is important for teachers to not let this bad mood carry over into their attitude. This can be a difficult thing to do. We are only human after all. When you are feeling like you are in a bad mood before you even get to school, try to make an effort *ahead of time* to not let this affect the way that you will handle discipline. Taking a proactive approach in this way can go a long way in keeping your emotions out of your discipline procedures.

TEACHER TIP
How to Handle Stress and Anxiety in the Middle of Class

Sometimes even teachers can get a little stage fright or have panic set in. Many people experience a little fear when speaking in public, even teachers. Most teachers will eventually figure out a way to deal with this issue.

The larger threat to stress levels for teachers is having misbehaviors occur and having the feeling of not being able to handle them. This can happen either as the result of an unexpected situation or even as just a *fear* that something unexpected might happen. Whether teachers choose to use the plan in this book or another one of their own, just having something planned and ready for difficult situations can bring peace of mind.

---

19. Use an Alphabetical Seating Chart

Using alphabetical seating charts means that papers are automatically in order when they are passed in. Having papers in order saves time, effort, and therefore stress. Also, changing a seating arrangement for a student because of misbehavior means that the teacher is adjusting to *the student*. Instead, the students should be the ones who have to adjust to the *teacher*. Having to change seating arrangements is admitting that the original classroom management plan did not work.

20. Keep Calm for as Long as Possible

Keeping calm is not only a good idea for dealing with classroom management, but it is also a wise approach to take in other teaching situations as well. Whether the issue is stage fright, an observation, making mistakes in front of students, or any other possible problem, staying calm is almost always the best course of action.

Old School: Successful teachers get themselves geared up emotionally to be able to sustain an aggressive and unfriendly attitude until they decide that it is safe to let up.

New School: Successful teachers mentally prepare themselves to be under control and unemotional.

It is actually possible to reach a point where there is little or no concern about student misbehavior. Using the New Style of classroom management can go a long way toward helping teachers reach that goal. There is no need for teachers to worry and dread the time that students might misbehave. Being prepared for any situation can go a long way toward reducing the stress that comes with uncertainty about misbehavior in the classroom.

The fear of students misbehaving and having no answer for it is one of the biggest causes of stress for teachers. Being organized and prepared is a great way to overcome this issue. When teachers let students cause stress because of bad behavior they are giving the students power over them. Life is too short to let misbehaving students ruin a good day, school year, or career!

Key Points

- Teaching is a stressful job. However, steps can be taken to dramatically reduce the amount of stress that teachers have to face.
- Some strategies for stress reduction are the same as they would be for other jobs: exercise, eat right, get plenty of sleep, and so forth.
- Teachers should do their best to have a separate life away from school. Living at least twenty miles away can help accomplish this goal.
- Taking breaks away from teaching is extremely important. Teachers who want to avoid burnout should strongly consider not teaching or tutoring during the summer break.
- Efficiency in grading is essential to lowering stress. Teachers who need help in this area would be wise to ask other teachers for help.
- Using anger and intimidation to keep order is an unnecessary strategy that can cause heavy amounts of stress.
- Thorough and detailed plans are always great for stress reduction.

6

Getting Along with Other Teachers

Nature Hath Framed Strange Fellows in Her Time

To get respect you have to give it.

—from the movie *Freedom Writers*

One of the most important things that teachers can do is to try to have positive relationships with their fellow teachers. Teaching is difficult enough without adding stress to the job because of an issue with a coworker. It seems like some teachers go out of their way to look for conflict. There is no reason to add tension to an already stressful job! Sometimes disagreements are unavoidable, but most of the difficulty caused by disputes with other teachers can be eliminated.

How to Have Good Relationships with Coworkers

1. Avoid Being Competitive

The goal for teachers should be to get the best out of themselves and their students, not to compete with other teachers. If competition is a goal, then it should definitely not be made known.

Quoted from *The Merchant of Venice*.

2. Be Humble

Teachers should not look down on their coworkers for any reason. Things like experience, subject taught, degrees attained, and so on should not be used as excuses for arrogance. Every teacher thinks that his or her class is the most important one in the school and a lot may think that they are the best teacher. It may be alright to think any of those things, but they should definitely never be communicated.

3. Be Willing to Admit When Wrong

So many arguments can be avoided if one side can admit that he or she is wrong and take responsibility. Sometimes errors in judgment are made. Most mistakes are not the end of the world. Taking responsibility for mistakes and being willing to admit when wrong will earn respect from coworkers.

4. Be Cooperative

Most schools have teachers with a wide variety of knowledge and experience. Hoarding a good idea for the sake of competition is selfish (especially when it comes to classroom management!). There is no need to be pushy, but sharing helpful information can make a huge difference when it comes to the success of a school. This is especially true for new teachers who may be shy about asking for help.

PERSONAL EXPERIENCE
Getting Along with Coworkers

I have always managed to do a good job of being friendly with my coworkers. When you teach for as many years as I have, though, some disputes are sure to come up. While I do not have any stories that are too dramatic, I have certainly witnessed plenty of conflict. I have seen entire departments have disputes with other ones (i.e., the English teachers versus the social studies teachers) and I have seen conflicts within departments tear them apart. These conflicts are never good for teachers, which in turn makes them not good for students.

---

5. Be Slow to Involve Administration in Disputes

There are few things more insulting than being tattled on to the boss. Teachers should handle disputes like adults and try to work them out individually first. Getting facts straight in a disagreement and avoiding a confrontational attitude are keys. The boss should not be involved unless every attempt for reconciliation has already been made.

6. Do Not Leave School with an Unresolved Issue

Just like married couples should never go to bed upset, teachers should try to never leave school angry with a coworker. Unresolved conflict just makes things worse and raises tension. The sooner the conflict is resolved, the better.

7. Do Not Gossip about Other Teachers

Some teachers always seem to be tempted to talk about students, administrators, and their fellow teachers. Gossip of any kind is extremely bad manners. Teachers would be wise to never name names of other people at the school for any reason publicly. This goes for teachers, students, and other school employees.

Negative Consequences of Coworker Conflict

- Increased stress
- Negative atmosphere
- Sides being formed—lack of unity
- A decrease in productivity and learning
- A decrease in teacher cooperation and sharing of ideas

What to Do When Your Rules Are Different from Other Teachers at Your School

Teachers who are willing to make a change to teach in the New Style will automatically be different from a lot of their fellow teachers. The reason is that most teachers today are still caught up in the old ways of handling classroom discipline. When this occurs, teachers using the New Style should not antagonize their coworkers for using the old ways. The best way to handle this kind of situation is to simply tell them how the New Style has been helpful.

Most people do not like change. There are some teachers out there who will resist anything new no matter how well it may work. If the New Style of discipline proves to be successful, it should not be kept secret! The New Style for classroom management is intended to be shared and perfected among teachers!

Old School: Teachers should keep everything to themselves so that they can stand apart from their coworkers and help their own reputations.

New School: Teachers should do whatever they can to form and protect good relationships with their coworkers to make the school environment as positive as possible.

TEACHER TIP
Never Call Other Teachers by Their First Name in Front of Students

Little things are important when it comes to encouraging an atmosphere of student respect for teachers. Using first names is an easy way for students to disrespect their teachers. Some administrators may even recommend not using just the last name as a greeting (i.e., "Hey, Smith"). This rule may seem excessive, but every little effort can make an impact when it comes to encouraging student respect. With student respect for teachers not being an automatic for many young people, every attempt to improve it is helpful.

Key Points

- Getting along well with coworkers can be a great way to reduce stress for teachers.
- Teachers should have a spirit of cooperation with each other, not competition.
- Disputes among teachers should be handled as quickly as possible. Letting them continue for days often escalates tension.
- Talking about other teachers and students is unprofessional. This practice should be avoided if at all possible.
- Teachers who use the New Style of teaching should share it!

7

Dealing with Parents

Mind Your Speech a Little Lest You Should Mar Your Fortunes

Wake up and smell the coffee, Mrs. Bueller. It's a fool's paradise. He is just leading you down the primrose path.

—from the movie *Ferris Bueller's Day Off*

The Relationship between Teachers and Parents

The topic of parent/teacher relations can be a tricky one. Having to deal with parents can sometimes be very unpleasant for teachers. Some avoid it as much as possible for fear of getting themselves into trouble. For present-day teachers to be successful, though, they need to stop thinking of parents as the enemy.

The relationship between a teacher and the parents of their students is always a little tricky. To be successful, teachers must deal with parents as if they are on the same side. In almost all situations, both the parents and teachers have a common goal: the well-being and success of the student. But there are some issues present in the nature of the relationship that can lead to conflict.

Quoted from *King Lear*.

Why Teachers and Parents Sometimes Have Conflict

Even with every intention of cooperation, teachers and parents can easily find themselves in conflict. There are a few reasons why this conflict can occur.

1. Miscommunication

Miscommunication can easily happen between parents and teachers because they are not often face to face. In most cases, parents are usually limited to what their child tells them. As a result, the description of events can often be inaccurate, either on purpose or by accident. Students have been known to exaggerate, leave out key pieces of information, or flat out fabricate events to save themselves from punishment. Also, students will almost always describe their actions in a positive light in any dispute. As a result, there are many times when teachers get undeserved criticism.

2. Both Sides Are Used to Being in Positions of Power and Control

Let's face it, parents and teachers are both used to having power when it comes to students. As a result, either one may feel threatened when the other tries to take control. As much as teachers may not like to admit it, however, parents are ultimately the ones who make the final decisions. Parents, however, should also realize that teachers are the ones in control when the child is in the classroom. They need to learn to trust teachers and school administration when it comes to doing what is best for their child. It is very important that both sides remember that they have the success of the child as their common goal.

3. Both Sides Have Differing Opinions about What Is Best for the Child

This can be a very difficult situation. As was stated earlier, parents have the ultimate decision-making power over what happens regarding their child. The problem comes when the two sides do not agree on the best course of action. Parents may think they always know what is right, but they are not always experts when it comes to education. Sometimes parents just have to trust the expertise of the teachers and school officials. Parents trust professionals when it comes to fixing cars, flying planes, giving medical care, and so forth. They should do the same with teachers.

4. Parents Go Over the Head of the Teacher and Complain to an Administrator

If parents want to find a way to totally disrespect a teacher, this is the way to do it. Of course, there are times when a parent would have a legitimate reason to go to an administrator. This should only happen for very extreme cases, however, such as when the safety of the child is at risk. Most of the time, though, parents could easily solve their issues with teachers on their own, without having to bring in outside help. Bringing in administrators or school officials to handle problems that are anything but extreme is very insulting to teachers.

5. Parents May Have Formed Negative Opinions about Teachers from Their Own Time as Students

Teachers would be wise to realize that many parents may have had bad experiences in school with teachers themselves. Maybe they had a teacher who gave them a failing grade, or had them kicked out of school, or made their life miserable in some way or another. With that kind of past, it is easy to see why these parents may not be willing to just jump right in with everything the teacher says. As a result, every parent is not necessarily going to automatically be on the side of the teacher. In fact, many parents may need to be convinced why they should not be *against* the teacher.

6. Parents Sometimes Expect the Teacher to Raise Their Child for Them

Unfortunately, there are some parents out there who expect teachers to transform their children from brats into perfect angels. These parents seem to feel that it is the teacher's job to not only teach, but to raise their children for them. If children misbehave, then they think it must be the teacher's fault. While this attitude may not be common, it definitely exists.

Teachers are exposed to this attitude when they call parents to discuss misbehavior of the child and the response is something like "Well, they do not behave well at home either. It is your job to make them behave at school." Yikes. It is best for teachers dealing with these kinds of parents to just do the best they can and avoid any interaction with them. There will not likely be any reasonable discussion.

7. Parents See a Complaint from a Teacher as an Attack on Their Ability to Raise Children

This is another reason why teachers should be very careful with the way they interact with parents. There is no reason to come across as insulting. Teachers should criticize the child's misbehavior and not make it sound like they are insulting the child personally. Parents often think that an insult of their children is an insult of their child-raising ability. When teachers go out of their way to be respectful to parents, they have a much better chance of getting cooperation. This is especially true if teachers can make positive comments about the student. Anything that can be done to show parents respect is beneficial.

8. The Teacher Actually Did Something to Deserve the Conflict

As much as teachers may hate to admit it, there may be times when they actually do deserve blame for something. When this occurs, it is best for teachers to apologize and move on. There is no need for excessive apologizing or groveling, but teachers do need to be clear about their regret and be accountable. If done quickly, this gesture can go a long way toward diffusing any conflict.

TEACHER TIP
Imagine Yourself in the Place of the Parent

When dealing with parents, teachers should always try to picture their students as if they were their own children. Believe it or not, these students are not just there to test and bother you. Your students are somebody's children. Always try to be calm and slow to anger when dealing with parents. In those rare instances when a parent looks like they may start to become belligerent, be sure to have another teacher or administrator present. You do not want to be in a position where parents are accusing you of saying or doing something and have it become a situation of your word against theirs.

The Role of Parents in the New Style of Discipline

Parents should not be counted on for help in changing a student's bad conduct in class! Teachers are more likely to get help from parents when it comes to improving a student's grade but not their behavior. This is a major change for teachers compared with those in past generations. Teachers can no longer solely rely on parental influence to affect behavior at school. If parents do something to help change behavior of their child, then that is a bonus. This does not mean to say that no parent can ever help a teacher with misbehavior. The point is that teachers cannot *expect* this help.

Old School: Parents should be counted on to help change a misbehaving student's bad behavior.

New School: Parent contact should be made to *notify* parents but not to expect them to have any impact on the student's behavior.

Tips for Talking to Parents

Always respond quickly—Teachers should try to show respect to parents as much as possible. Small gestures like responding quickly to phone calls and e-mails from parents can go a long way to building a good relationship with them.

Communicate early—Parents should be aware of what is going on in their child's class. Sending home a copy of the grading and discipline plan for the class is wise. Early communication is especially important for teachers who are planning on handling discipline with the New Style discussed in this book. Teachers should always get the signature of parents in case there is ever a need for proof of communication.

Stay calm during disputes—Parents may get angry if a teacher says or does something negative. In these cases, it is important for the teacher to stay calm for as long as possible. If parents feel the need to use profanity, teachers of course should not be tempted to respond with similar behavior. Many times when students misbehave it is because their parents are exhibiting the same behavior at home. Teachers should make their points to parents as calmly as possible and make a compromise if appropriate. Of course, teachers should always stand firm for what they believe is right and never take verbal abuse. A parent never has the right to try to intimidate a teacher.

Interacting with Parents

I want to be very clear that I am not trying to insult parents in this chapter. Parents have a right to know everything that is going on in their child's life. They ultimately have the final say in every decision that affects their child.

The main difference in dealing with parents in the New Style of classroom management is that parents can no longer be counted on to correct a child's behavior. This is not an insult to parents; it is just a sign of the times. Children respect adults less as a whole than they used to, including their parents.

The ideas in this book are not meant to exclude parents from decision making or information about the education of their children. The point is more to lower teachers' expectations that parent involvement can be counted on as a great solution for their classroom management plans.

Teachers should always be very careful with what they say to parents. It is the job of teachers to serve students, and parents often have a very important role in the lives of their children. This respect should be given regardless of the age of the teacher. As teachers get older, they sometimes face the challenge of being older than the principal, parents, and other staff. Older teachers cannot let this age difference affect the way they treat parents.

There is always a line that parents should not cross, of course. There is never a reason for teachers to become doormats to anyone. Parents are not the boss of the teachers and they do not have power over them. They do deserve to be involved in the education of their children, however, and this right should be respected.

Key Points

- The relationship between teachers and parents is extremely important. Teachers cannot view parents as the enemy.
- Much of the conflict that happens between parents and teachers is the result of miscommunication and misunderstanding.
- Both parents and teachers are used to being in positions of control. They would both be wise to try to be as understanding as possible with each other.
- Parents are not always comfortable dealing with teachers. Many may have had bad experiences during their time as students.
- Teachers should communicate with parents when something is going on that they should know about. The days when teachers could count on parents to help with classroom management are over.
- Parents may occasionally become belligerent with teachers. When this happens, teachers should do their best to stay calm, and they should *always* have an administrator present when there is the potential for conflict.

8

A Word to Administrators

Uneasy Lies the Head That Wears a Crown

> It's almost funny. I got dragged into this gig kicking and screaming, and now it's the only thing I want to do.
>
> —from the movie *Mr. Holland's Opus*

Principals have extremely tough jobs. That fact is true no matter the grades, sizes, locations, or socioeconomic levels of the surrounding communities of their schools. While some administrative jobs may be more difficult than others, they are all very demanding. The responsibilities are great and the hours never end. People who devote themselves to being principals should be highly commended.

Running a school and handling teachers is very much like a business. Businesses are most successful when the employees are put in the best situations to succeed. Great business owners realize that employees are most productive when they are happiest and reaching their potential. The same idea is true for teachers. Principals who make an effort to put their teachers in the best situations for success are the ones who will have the best

---

Quoted from *Henry IV*.

schools. It is as simple as that. The challenge for administrators is to figure out how to make this happen.

How Administrators Can Put Teachers in the Best Situations for Success

1. Give Teachers as Much Freedom as Possible

Once boundaries are set, employees will thrive when they are given freedom. The best way for principals to show respect for their teachers is to give them as much power and control as possible. In most cases the more freedom teachers have the better off they and the school will be.

Most teachers will respond to an appropriate amount of freedom with their best effort. Some may try to take advantage of this kind of control, but principals will be able to recognize this abuse quickly. If teachers are good enough to be hired, then they should be given a chance to work without having the boss look over their shoulder. Micromanaging teachers and taking away their authority rarely works well.

2. Support Teachers When Parents Complain (Unless They Have Done Something *Really* Bad)

Many principals used to be teachers themselves, so they should remember how difficult the job can be. Teaching is hard enough without having to deal with a principal who is not supportive in disputes with parents. Unless teachers have clearly done something wrong, the administrator should do everything possible to be on the side of teachers. Even when a situation may look bad, no "side" should be taken until there is irrefutable evidence of wrongdoing.

When principals automatically take the parents' side in a dispute, they weaken the teacher's authority. The natural authority of a teacher is very important; principals should always keep this in mind. If administrators weaken this authority by publicly doubting their teachers, then they will likely cripple their effectiveness with students.

3. Let Teachers Work in Their Strengths

The only way that principals will get the maximum performance from their teachers is if they allow them to work in their strengths. Administrators who have been coaches can probably relate best to this statement. Football coaches do not take their heaviest players and put them at quarterback. Basketball coaches do not take the seven foot player and make him the point guard. The same approach should be used in a school.

Principals should make an effort to find out what teachers love to teach, what they hate to teach, and everything in between. They do not have to promise to let teachers get every class they want, but taking teachers' likes and dislikes into consideration during class scheduling does wonders for a school. While it is obvious that not all teachers can have every class they want on their schedule, most teachers do best when they can teach subjects that fit their talents and interests.

Old School: Principals should create teachers' schedules based on seniority, habit, and chance.

New School: Principals should find out where their teachers have the most interest and ability and create class schedules with this information in mind.

---

4. Show Respect and Avoid Treating Teachers like Students

Principals who treat teachers like students will not bring out their best. In many cases, principals may have come from a background of teaching before becoming administrators. As a result, they may not be used to dealing with adults in a professional way. All they know is how to take control, use anger and attitude to establish discipline, and all of the other old methods that teachers use to deal with children. Therefore, they face the same issues as teachers themselves who try to use the old methods in classrooms.

If principals fall back into their old habits and start behaving like they did when they were teaching, they will quickly lose effectiveness. Adults do not do well when they are treated like children. Lack of respect for the boss is never good for productivity, and this will be the inevitable result if teachers are treated like students. Principals who want to get the best performance from their teachers should do whatever they can to show them respect.

5. Do Not Use Fear as a Motivator

The days of using fear as a primary motivator are over. Fear as a motivator can no longer work well with students, and the same is true for teachers. Administrators who keep their teachers in a constant state of fear will never get their best performance. One of the key traits of a good teacher is the ability to take control of a classroom. Many teachers are in the profession because they are comfortable having this kind of control. There is something in the personality of most teachers that makes them capable leaders. The same trait, however, can make them resistant to overmanagement.

Principals who try to take too much control will only frustrate and weaken the morale of their teachers. Clear-cut expectations and consequences for mistakes should be given to teachers just like students. Principals need to realize this concept when they are deciding how to deal with the management of their teachers. One of the worst things a principal can do is punish a teacher for breaking a rule that was not made clear ahead of time.

Of course, as in any job, employees cannot be allowed *complete* freedom. Principals need to be aware of what is going on as much as possible, and there should be clear boundaries and guidelines. In the end, however, teachers do best when they are allowed to have as much control as possible over their classrooms and schedules.

> **PERSONAL EXPERIENCE**
> **Principals Who Use Fear to Motivate**
>
> I have generally been lucky enough to have had good principals during my fifteen years of teaching. I did hear from a friend of mine, however, about a principal who was always looking over the teachers' shoulders. This principal was consistently in the classrooms checking up on what the teachers were doing. If there was any dispute, he would always take the side of the parents and even students and assume the problem must have been the teacher's mistake. I cannot imagine having to work for a principal like that, but I know that they exist. Micromanaging and treating teachers like they are incompetent is no way to have a successful school.

6. Establish a List of Nonnegotiable Rules for Teachers

Communication and clarity are extremely important in the classroom and they are equally important for principals. Principals should decide what they expect from their teachers and communicate information. Some expectations will be nonnegotiable, absolute requirements (i.e., a time deadline for getting to school) and some may not be absolute requirements (i.e., no drinking soda in class). It is not wise to say that every expectation is nonnegotiable. In some matters principals may allow for some leeway while others must be locked in stone. Principals should post their most important, nonnegotiable rules for teachers as well.

7. Remember What It Was Like to Be a Teacher

As mentioned earlier, most administrators were teachers at some point, although for some it may have been a very long time ago. If they want to be successful leaders, principals need to remember what it was like when they were in the classroom. When they were teaching, these principals likely did not appreciate a boss who was breathing down their neck and requiring excessive amounts of paper work. They probably did not like a principal who quickly took the side of the parents and students over the teachers. If current administrators stop and think about how it was for them during their teaching days, they may have a little more appreciation for their teachers and what they go through.

8. Don't Insist That Teachers Do Everything the Old Way

Administrators who insist on having things done like they were in the old days will be left behind. Times change. The best way of doing things thirty years ago is not necessarily the best method for success today. Students and parents have more power and more voice than they ever had. Also, there are more distractions for students than there were in the past. Teachers and administrators need to adjust to this change in the nature of education and be ready to transform their methods.

9. Be Open to Communication with Teachers

Principals who do not keep an open channel of communication with their teachers and other employees are inviting problems. If teachers have no outlet to voice their concerns, the result will be behind-the-scenes griping and resentment. Ultimately, principals make the final decisions, but showing respect for teachers and listening to their opinions will encourage a much more positive school environment. It will also give teachers more ownership in the school if they feel like their opinions are heard. Teachers do best when they feel appreciated.

TEACHER TIP
Be Willing to Communicate with Your Principal!

Teachers who have concerns or problems should make an attempt to communicate with the principal. It is not a good idea to keep problems in and let them build up and cause frustration. This communication can be in person, by phone, e-mail, or whatever it takes. The method is not important.

This advice should not be overused, of course. Principals do not have the time to take care of every little problem teachers may face. Teachers should not feel like they are alone when a significant problem occurs, however.

Key Points

- Schools are like businesses. Principals would be wise to think this way.
- Principals should find out what their teachers' strengths and interests are so that they can be put in the best situations for success.
- Many teachers enjoy control and autonomy. Too much micromanaging and supervision by administrators can be detrimental to the teachers' success.
- Many administrators come from a teaching background. They should be careful to not treat their teachers like children and remember how it felt to be a teacher.
- Fear is not a great motivator for teachers.
- Administrators would be wise to encourage open communication with their teachers.

9

Adjusting the Plan for College Classrooms

I Bear a Charmed Life

> You come in here with a skull full of mush and you
> leave thinking like a lawyer.
>
> —from the movie *The Paper Chase*

The New Style of classroom management proposed in this book is intended for classes from the eighth grade level all the way to college level. Classroom management can be a difficult issue for college professors just as much as it can be for high school and middle school teachers. This is especially true when teaching freshmen in college who still may be used to behaving like they did in high school. It is a foolish mistake for college professors to think that students will automatically behave well just because they are in college. There may be some adjustments needed when applying the New Style in college classrooms, but the basic principles are still the same for all age levels.

Quoted from *Macbeth*.

How Classroom Management Is the Same in College

1. Clear Rules and Consequences Are Still Needed

The nature of the rules and consequences may be slightly different in college, but they are still needed. College professors, however, may be able to get away with very few rules compared to high school teachers. They may have a list of one sentence rules like "no interrupting, do not be late, and no eating in class." Their consequences may be either removal from class for the day or permanently. As long as the severity of the consequence is close to the severity of the misbehavior, consequences can be effective. Sometimes many different consequences are not needed to accomplish this goal.

There is no need for professors to have a large number of rules in college. They can put up with much less student misbehavior than high school and middle school teachers. College professors simply need to think of two or three misbehaviors that they definitely want to eliminate and then come up with a simple consequence or two to use. Having fewer things to worry about can make the management plan much easier to enforce.

Old School: College professors do not have to worry about classroom management. The students will automatically behave.

New School: College professors need to have a basic classroom management plan in place just in case students have retained some bad behavior habits from high school.

---

2. There Is Still No Reason to Use Anger or Intimidation as Tools for Classroom Management

Most college professors have figured this out already. There is no need to use anger when there are other effective possibilities available. Since professors are able to kick a student out of class whenever they feel the need, they usually do not have to rely on anger and intimidation to accomplish successful classroom management. College professors have a great advantage over high school teachers for this reason. They also demonstrate one of the main points of this book: classroom management can be effective when consequences are clear and uncomfortable enough for the students.

3. Misbehaving Students Can Still Ruin a College Class If They Are Not Dealt With Effectively

No matter the grade level, from eighth grade to college, a class can be ruined by misbehaving students who are not dealt with effectively. This is why the New Style discussed in this book is so important. Classes of all levels and age groups must be made to behave so that learning can be maximized.

PERSONAL EXPERIENCE
Too Much Talking in Class

I remember taking an elective course in college that had some student behavior issues. For whatever reason, there was often a lot of talking that went on during that class. The professor would occasionally ask for quiet, but he never really did anything about it. I am sure that this professor would have preferred that there be less talking. He just did not have any recourse to deal with the situation.

There are rarely, if ever, times in college classes that extreme misbehaviors occur. However, occasionally there are times when talking is excessive. Professors should be ready to handle those situations and decide what they will do ahead of time instead of in the heat of the moment. An organized, proactive plan is always the best choice.

How Classroom Management Is Different in College

1. Students Are More Willing to Participate in Class

College professors have an advantage that also exists for coaches: most of the students *choose* to be enrolled. As a result, professors can use this information to their advantage. When students want to be there, the professor can then use the threat of loss of class time (and grade) as an effective consequence. Therefore, students always know in the back of their minds that the professor has the power to get rid of them, even permanently. High school and middle school teachers have similar power to an extent, but the misbehavior has to be *much* worse at those levels for teachers to be able to remove someone from class.

2. Parents Are Much Less of an Influence

In most cases in college, the parents are hundreds of miles or more away. Professors do not have to be as concerned about parents getting involved as high school teachers do. By the time they get to college, students have to learn how to handle their own issues. Parents are often still paying the bills, but the students must now speak for themselves. As a result, professors do not have to consider parental response nearly as much as high school teachers do when implementing their classroom management plans.

3. Cheating Usually Has Much More Serious Consequences in College

If a student gets caught cheating on a test in high school, the punishment is often a failing grade on the test. If a student is caught cheating in college, the result would likely be expulsion from school. This is quite a difference in consequences! As a result, student dishonesty is much less prevalent in college. Cheating is still a threat there, but students are definitely not as frivolous about it as they are in high school. The threat of expulsion is a very strong deterrent in college.

When College Students Do Not Know Any Better

Since behavior in high schools seems to be getting worse, many students bring bad habits along with them to college. Professors of classes containing mostly freshmen need to be prepared to deal with students who do not know how to behave appropriately. Either these students have never been taught, or they have never been made to follow rules. As a result, college professors should be prepared for potential misbehavior from these students. If they can catch disruptions early on and put a stop to it, professors can help students make a much smoother transition from high school to college. Professors can benefit greatly from using the New Style because they still need to address less severe disruptions.

TEACHER TIP
Do Not Be Too Quick to Judge Incoming Freshmen

Incoming freshmen should know how to act in a classroom. The reality, though, is that some of them may not have been expected to behave well in high school. Many high school teachers today are only going through the motions without an effective plan for classroom management. They take the attitude that if there are no extreme misbehaviors then everything is fine. There is too much of this acceptance of mediocrity in schools today.

As a result, college professors should realize that they may need to train some of the incoming freshmen about appropriate classroom behavior. It may mean that some students have to learn the hard way and get kicked out of class a time or two (without excessive anger or intimidation, of course!). Most students should still be fine when it comes to behaving well in a classroom, but there could very well be a large number who still need a little training.

Key Points

- The New Style of classroom management can be used for college classes.
- Communication about rules is especially important for college students.
- Anger and intimidation works even less on college students than it does on younger ones.
- Parents play much less of a role in classroom management in college than they do in high school. This can be both good and bad for the instructor.
- Many freshmen who are entering college may not have gone to a high school that emphasized appropriate classroom behavior. These students may need even more communication and training than other students.

10

Using the Plan in Coaching Situations

Some Are Born Great, Some Achieve Greatness, and Some Have Greatness Thrust Upon Them

> This is no democracy. It is a dictatorship. I am the law.
>
> —from the movie *Remember the Titans*

The New Style of discipline can be applied to coaching sports as well. The basic ideas are the same as they are in classrooms. Coaches need to realize, just like teachers, that times have changed and that players and parents have more power than they used to have. Because of this increase in power, behavior management for coaches needs to be organized and reasonable just as it does for classroom teachers. There are a few advantages and disadvantages that coaches have over classroom teachers when it comes to management.

Quoted from *Twelfth Night*.

Advantages That Coaches
Have Over Classroom Teachers

1. Most of the Players Want to Be There

Having players who have volunteered to play a sport is a huge advantage that coaches have over classroom teachers. Most players in a given sport are there because they want to play. Coaches can use this desire to their advantage when it comes to choosing consequences for misbehaviors. Few things send a message to a player better than being forced to spend time on the bench.

While some students do want to be successful in the classroom, most are not in there dying to learn. A teacher who threatened to teach less would probably be cheered in most classrooms. This is where the main difference occurs between teaching and coaching. The threat of loss of participation is a great option for coaches that teachers do not usually have at their disposal.

2. There Are Many More Consequences Available for Coaches

Player management can be much easier to implement for coaches because of the ease in finding reasonable consequences for less extreme offenses. One of the biggest challenges for teachers is finding potential consequences that match the severity of the smaller misbehavior issues. Coaches, on the other hand, have a wide range of possibilities for these situations. For instance, using running as a consequence for misbehavior can be very useful for coaches because there are so many different methods and amounts that can be required.

Depending on the severity of the misbehavior, coaches can have players run anything from a short sprint to a number of miles. The possibilities are endless. With such a range of severity for the consequences, coaches can easily find appropriate ones for the range of possible misbehaviors. This flexibility is an option that most classroom teachers do not have.

TEACHER TIP
Choosing Consequences When Coaching

The selection of consequences is very important when coaching a team. The players need to know what consequences will result for different misbehaviors. The coach should have a combination of consequences for specific behaviors (i.e., an unexcused miss of practice means running two miles) and general consequences for things that may come up. The general consequences should be assigned to general severities of possible misbehaviors rather than specific ones. Whether the consequences chosen will be varieties of extra running, missed game time, suspensions, or anything else, coaches need to have a clear plan for consequences before the season begins.

3. Coaches Often Have Players for Multiple Years

Coaches often have players on their teams for two to four years. As a result, they can teach players exactly what is expected of them. The rules and consequences become established so that the coach does not have to spend much time going over them. Also, players with more experience can warn the newer players about what to do and not to do. Most teachers have to start from scratch every time a new class begins since they will be teaching new groups of students each time.

4. Head Coaches Often Have Assistants

Having assistants can help the head coach be more consistent and effective when implementing the team behavior management plan. Assistants are also good for providing feedback and other perspectives for decisions about appropriate rules and consequences. They also make record keeping much easier.

Disadvantages for Coaches Compared to Classroom Teachers

1. There Are No Grades

Teachers will still have many students who behave well because they know that the teacher has the power over their grades. Students who are looking ahead to college and career choices will be more likely to behave well in the classroom. This is an option that coaches do not have.

2. Players Can Quit Much More Easily

Since playing a sport is a volunteer activity, some players will not take the commitment seriously. As soon as they lose playing time or do not like the coach, these players will quit the team without a second thought. This situation is more prevalent today than it used to be, most likely because young people are more used to getting their way. Many young people today are also not getting as much parental encouragement to stick with their commitments.

The threat of players quitting in revolt of a harsh or unfair coach also has to enter the decision-making process when formulating the team management plan. This problem is even more serious today because of the increasing pressure for coaches to win. Students do quit school occasionally, but it is much less frequent and a more serious issue. Many players will quit a team without hesitation for very little reason. Teachers do not have to worry about this problem nearly as much as coaches.

3. Games Are Public

Since games are public, coaches are a little more "under the microscope" than classroom teachers. The way they handle player management is often out in the open for everyone to see, at least on game day. As a result, coaches have a little more accountability to be fair and reasonable to students than teachers have. This also means that it is even more important for coaches to avoid using emotion when handling behavior issues.

Essential Parts of a Successful Coaching Behavior Management Plan

1. Clear Organization

Coaches need to have their behavior plans clearly defined before the season begins. One of the worst things coaches can do is try to make up rules and consequences as they go. This does not mean that there should be a specific consequence for every rule that might be broken. Instead, there should be a set of possible consequences for small to medium infractions and another set for major infractions. Players should be made aware of these rules and consequences from the beginning. Some coaches may even want to involve some or all of the players in developing the list of rules and consequences. Involving the players in the decision making gives validity to the rules and consequences that would not otherwise exist.

However a coach decides to develop the team management plan, the rules and consequences should be made clear to players before the season begins. They should be required to take the plan home and sign it along with their parents. Parents should be aware of any behavior management plan that is being used. When parents are notified ahead of time about consequences for behavior issues for players, they have no room to complain if their children are fairly punished.

PERSONAL EXPERIENCE
How Coaching Inspired the Invention of the New Style

I coached basketball during most of my teaching career, even as a student teacher. About half of that time I worked as an assistant, the other half as a head coach. When I was head coaching, I had discipline down to a science. I had the players acting like an army. They rarely did anything that I did not allow them to do.

My attempts at management in the classroom, however, did not go as well. I was mediocre at best at having the students behave how I wanted. I could not figure out how I could be so good at discipline in my coaching and not in the classroom. Then I had a great realization. The main difference was the ease that I had in finding appropriate consequences in coaching, while I could not do this when teaching. When I studied the difference in how I conducted my discipline plans in coaching and in the classroom, I realized that the implementation of consequences was the key. Once I discovered that information, I set out to figure out how to accomplish the same thing in the classroom. The results are found in this book.

2. Swift Enforcement of Consequences

The longer a coach waits to enforce a consequence, the less effective it will be. Coaches should not be tempted to delay consequences by keeping track of who owes what. Stopping the player immediately and enforcing the consequence is almost always the best course of action. If this cannot be done immediately, it should at least be taken care of as soon as possible.

3. A Professional Demeanor When Implementing Consequences

Just as in teaching, the method of using anger and intimidation for every misbehavior in coaching is becoming less and less effective. This method may have worked years ago, but its time is now past. Anger and intimidation should only be used for extreme misbehaviors. This does not mean that a coach cannot have a stern attitude. It simply means that coaches should not expect to get results by yelling at players over every little issue.

Even if coaches can use this aggressive method effectively, it only works if they continue it. Once a coach establishes that anger is what is required to get anything done, no other method will work. Having to be mean and angry all the time is no way to have to live all day, every day for an entire career. As is the case in teaching, this practice is asking for stress and eventual burnout.

4. Good Record Keeping

This piece of advice is probably common sense but it deserves mentioning. When coaches deal with a large number of players within a year or over many years, it is easy to lose consistency. Having a record can make it much easier to be fair with players. Also, it can be a hassle for coaches to remember what they have done in the past. Most coaches do want to be consistent with players, but accomplishing this goal is not always as easy as it sounds. Keeping detailed records of consequences and misbehaviors can help coaches become much more consistent and effective in their behavior management.

5. A Healthy Balance of Praise and Criticism

The idea of mixing praise with criticism is nothing new, but many people in leadership positions seem to forget or ignore this concept. Leaders who do nothing but criticize people will eventually wear down the very people they are trying to motivate. On the other hand, leaders who are nothing but sugar blowers and praise *everything* will also lose effectiveness. The wise leader uses a well-balanced blend of the two. Players need to know that the coach is on their side, but they also need to know that he has boundaries for them. It is up to the coach to figure out how to balance the two methods in a way that inspires players to work hard and maximize their abilities.

Old School: The best coaches are the ones who rule with an iron fist and get results through yelling, screaming, and belittling players.

New School: The best coaches are the ones who find a healthy balance of criticism and praise and go out of their way to be as fair as possible to their players.

---

6. Support for Teachers or Professors

Good coaches always try to support the teachers or professors of the players they coach. This not only helps the players learn that their education is important, but it also helps the coach have a good reputation at the school. Coaches who focus completely on their sport are doing their players a disservice.

Key Points

- Behavior management when coaching is sometimes easier and sometimes harder than it is when teaching in the classroom.
- One of the biggest advantages for coaches over classroom teachers is that the players have chosen to participate.
- Finding reasonable consequences that match the severity of the misbehavior is *much* easier in coaching.
- Coaches often have the advantage of assistants working for them who can help handle some of the workload that comes with successful behavior management.
- Coaching is much more of a public situation than classroom teaching. This means more pressure on coaches when they are handling student misbehaviors in plain view of the public.
- Coaches who are in the habit of criticizing or getting emotional with players need to be sure to mix praise with the negative responses as much as possible.

11

A Word to New Teachers

Look Like the Innocent Flower, but Be the Serpent Under't

> This is what I have picked to do with my life!
>
> —from the movie *Dangerous Minds*

The first few months (and even years) in the teaching profession can be a very scary and intimidating time. No matter how well a new teacher's college career or student teaching went, there will still be many unexpected and stressful situations that will occur on the job. The teaching profession is definitely not easy and everyone is not cut out for it. The people who become teachers because of the great summer vacation time and long Christmas breaks will not last long. Trying to be a teacher without having the right character traits will quickly wear a person out. There is a certain kind of personality needed to be a capable teacher. It is definitely a calling and not just a job.

There are steps that can be taken by new teachers to lessen the difficulty of those first few days and months in the classroom. There is no way to completely eliminate all of the stress involved, of course, but a lot of it can be reduced. Some of the

---

Quoted from *Macbeth*.

advice listed in this chapter has already been mentioned previously, but much of it is worth repeating in reference to new teachers. Veteran teachers may benefit from it as well.

PERSONAL EXPERIENCE
The Kind of Personality Needed to Be a Teacher

Many times when people hear that I am a teacher, they say something like "I would not have the patience to do that job!" I never really considered myself to be a person with excessive amounts of patience either, but I do seem to have enough of it to be able to teach. Patience is not something so generalized that you either have it or you don't. People can have large amounts of one kind of patience but be low in other kinds. Potential teachers should not automatically eliminate the teaching idea just because they do not think they have unlimited amounts of patience.

There are many situations in life when I do not have patience. For instance, I do not feel patient when I am standing in lines, waiting for my food at a restaurant, or listening to babies cry in a movie theater. I do, however, have the kind of patience needed for teaching. I learned that good teachers know to not get too upset at the little things. They do not worry so much about what students think of them, and they do not throw fits over every little rule that is broken. Teachers who worry excessively about these things quickly wear themselves out and have a very stressful time teaching.

Teachers have to be able to handle stress and unexpected situations with grace and poise. Developing abilities of awareness and alertness is also very important. When there are thirty students for which teachers are responsible, they cannot afford to let their guards down. Bad teachers are often oblivious to what is taking place in the classroom. Sometimes they even use this lack of attention as a defense against having to deal with student misbehavior. These are the kinds of classrooms that can become disastrous.

My usual responses to people who ask how I can teach are usually (1) I am somehow cut out for it, and (2) you have to be a little crazy to do it. Both are true.

The Importance of Having Mentors

Many school systems today have formal mentor programs in place, which allow incoming teachers to get used to how various things are done at the school. If there is not an official program for this, it is a good idea to find one or more teachers to help fill this role. The best mentors are teachers who are in the same department, but this is in no way a requirement. Starting out in a new school is difficult enough without having to figure out how everything is done there.

Five Things That Must Be True If Teaching Is a Calling

Teaching is not a job for everyone; it takes a certain kind of personality. Those who do it for the summers off, or to be able to coach a sport, are going to have problems. Many people feel like they know what teaching will be like because they were once on the other side as students. Most people who have only been students, however, have *no idea* what it is like to be a teacher. Some teachers make things look easier than they are, from handling classroom management to subject knowledge. Potential teachers should be very careful when deciding if they have the right kind of personality to get into the profession. It is not as easy as their old teachers made it look.

Five Qualities That All Teachers Should Have

1. A love of young people (particularly whatever age is being taught)
2. A love and mastery of the subject being taught
3. Extreme self-control
4. Ability to handle power
5. No desire to make a lot of money

The Importance of the First Day

The first day of a new school year or semester is very important for new teachers. The reason is that students will already have ideas about them that will have to be overcome. New teachers should be very careful to not get too close to students. Their roles are completely different from those of the students, of course, even though there may only be a few years' difference in age. These roles need to be defined and reinforced early on.

Students will often assume that they can push new teachers around because of the small difference in age. Students often think younger teachers will automatically be weaker than older ones. As a result, these teachers should make a point to show from the beginning that they are in total control of their classrooms. Therefore, new teachers should be serious, act older, dress professionally, and do whatever it takes to be authoritative. New teachers have to do whatever they can to show that they are not there to play games. One of the worst things that new, young teachers can do is to try to be buddies with the students. Trying to be buddies will often undermine any authority that the new teachers may have originally had.

TEACHER TIP
Do Not Read *Too* Much into the Student Teaching Experience

Student teaching is a great practice for prospective teachers who want to find out if the career is for them. It should not be the only factor in this decision, however. I was lucky enough to have a great supervising teacher during my experience and she is a big reason why I am still teaching today. However, student teaching does not necessarily show a person everything he or she needs to know about a possible future in teaching.

One reason potential teachers should not read too much into the student teaching experience is that the classes they taught during the experience will usually have already been trained by the supervising teacher. The behavior of the students may be drastically good or bad and it would have had nothing to do with anything the student teacher did.

Second, students often will not give student teachers the same respect that they would a regular teacher, even one right out of college. This means that student teachers may already have two strikes against them when it comes to classroom management. As a result, classroom management during the student teaching experience may be more difficult than it would be during a regular teaching situation.

Finally, student teachers can sometimes be spoiled by the support they get from their supervising teachers. It may be a shock to some teachers once they are on their own in an actual teaching job. Unless a person's student teaching experience was unbearable, however, the decision to teach or not should not be based on the student teaching experience.

The Importance of Avoiding a Goal of Popularity

New teachers may be tempted to try to become buddies with students. They are similar in age with the students and probably have similar interests. However, attempts at popularity are a very bad idea. While it is fine to have a goal of getting along well with students, it is dangerous to get buddy-buddy with them. When popularity is a goal, it becomes too easy to compromise fairness and professionalism to try to reach it. Also, students will usually recognize when a teacher is concerned with being popular and manipulate them.

It can be very disheartening for teachers if students make their dislike for them obvious. These cases really test teachers' intentions of truly not worrying about popularity. There are no teachers that will be liked by everyone. It is a futile endeavor to try to achieve this kind of popularity. Some students will love the teacher, some will hate the teacher, and most will be somewhere in between. Teachers cannot waste time and energy worrying about winning students over. The best idea for teachers is to go about the business of teaching and let the students think what they want.

Ignoring the Out-of-Date Advice to "Be Mean at First and Lighten Up Later"

This piece of advice is one of the most harmful things being taught to developing teachers today. This strategy simply does not work as well as it used to. Unfortunately, many of the education professors teach future teachers as if they will be entering the same world of education that the professors themselves came from. As has been discussed earlier, nothing could be further from the truth. Times have changed. A clear, organized classroom management plan is what is needed now. There is no reason to play the "be mean at first and lighten up later" game anymore. It is a waste of time and energy.

The Importance of Consistency, Clarity, and Organization

New teachers should not try to get too complicated when it comes to developing their first classroom management plan. The only requirement is that it should be easy to understand and implement. Teachers are busy enough as it is; they do not need the extra burden of a complex discipline plan. There is no need to try to impress anyone with the complexity of a classroom management plan anyway. Results are all that matter.

Figuring Out an Efficient Grading Style Quickly

This advice is very important for new teachers. Teaching is difficult enough at first without having to struggle to find a grading plan that works. New teachers should not rest until they find a teacher at their school who can help them find a favorable grading system. Teachers in the same department are the best sources of help, but any teachers can be useful. Figuring out an efficient grading system can save teachers a *tremendous* amount of work and stress. Also, having to change the grading system midway through a term is disastrous for teachers' credibility with students. It is best to have a good one ready from the beginning.

The Importance of Taking Home as Little Schoolwork as Possible

This advice may sound a little counterproductive. Many times new teachers will have additional responsibilities when they first start teaching. All teachers would be wise to take as little home as possible, but this is especially true for new teachers. In his book, *The Essential 55*, Ron Clark suggests that teachers occasionally take a break from doing schoolwork at home.

Most people have heard of the high turnover rate for teachers in the first four years. Not leaving schoolwork at school can be a large factor of this turnover rate. Taking work home will make teaching seem like it is a twenty-four-hour job, which quickly leads to burnout.

Coaching a Sport

Coaching can be a good way for new teachers to connect with students and the school in general. It can be time-consuming, but the commitment will usually be worth it. If the coaching position is as an assistant then the time requirement will not be too bad. Another benefit of coaching is that coaches are often excused from other less desirable teacher duties like serving on committees, hall monitoring after school, and so on. Being willing to coach can also be helpful in getting that first job!

Saying Yes to Everything Is a Bad Idea

This advice can sometimes be difficult to follow. Trying to be cooperative is good, but it is sometimes alright to say no. This is especially true if the request is for something that has to be done outside of school hours. Avoiding unnecessary stress is extremely important for teachers who are just starting out. Saying no takes some guts, depending on who is doing the asking, but learning to do so in a respectful way is a very valuable skill to develop.

The Importance of Getting Enough Sleep

Young teachers often feel like they can cut corners on sleep because they did so in college. A regular practice of seven or eight hours of sleep on school nights will go a long way toward helping performance in the classroom. Burning too much midnight oil can cause stress for teachers, as well as lessen their effectiveness during the school day. Also, getting enough sleep will usually increase teachers' patience and keep them from developing a short temper.

The Importance of Having an Outside Social Life

Teachers need to do everything they can to protect their mental health. Being consumed by the job can have disastrous results. Friends and family should not be neglected in favor of teaching duties. Also, single teachers should still try to have active social lives. Teachers can often get lonely, and they do not need any reason to have any thoughts of getting too close to a student. Married teachers and those with children should also make sure their families do not become less of a priority than schoolwork.

Supporting Students by Attending School Events

Students can tell if teachers are just going through the motions as they teach or if they actually care. Teachers should think of their students as more than just necessary evils to deal with in order to get a paycheck. Going to a few athletic and cultural events produced by the students goes a long way to forming stronger relationships with them. Students definitely notice these kinds of things.

Lesson Planning Should Be Done in Advance

Some principals require long and medium range lesson plans. If there is no formal requirement, however, lesson planning should still be done in at least one week blocks. Planning one day at a time can cause tremendous stress for teachers. There is something about having long-term direction that improves a teacher's organization and peace of mind. Sometimes last-minute planning cannot be helped, of course. As a rule, though, planning at least a few days ahead of time can be very helpful.

Grading and Paperwork
Should Be Completed Quickly

Seeing stacks of unfinished paperwork lying around can be very stressful. It may not always be possible to do everything as soon as it crosses the desk, but paperwork should be done as quickly as possible. There is something comforting about not having a mess in clear view on the desk. This suggestion may not sound like much, but every little thing that can be done to lower stress and frustration should be considered.

Not Believing Everything Education Professors Said

Education professors are very knowledgeable about a lot of topics. Classroom management is often not one of them. For one, many professors have not taught in a public school classroom in decades. Education has obviously changed a lot in that time. Hopefully college students know that it is OK to occasionally question things that professors tell them. Experienced teachers are a much more reliable source of information when it comes to what goes on in classrooms today.

Using Rewards to Motivate Is a Bad Idea
Unless Teaching Elementary School

There is a lot of classroom management advice that advocates using things like games, prizes, and parties to motivate students to behave. The idea is that if you are going to punish students, then you also have to reward them. This is a bad idea if the students are older. Older students will not be treated that way in college, and many of them will be there much faster than they realize. If teachers have an organized and efficient classroom management plan, there is no need to try to bribe students with rewards.

Showing Confidence Is Essential to Successful Classroom Management

One trait that teachers absolutely *must* show is confidence. Students are very good at gauging the confidence of their teachers. All teachers should be extremely confident in both the subject area they are teaching and in their classroom management plan as well. Hopefully, their college training will take care of the confidence in the subject matter. Confidence in classroom management may have to be developed, however.

When first starting out, teachers may not naturally have much confidence. If that is the case, they need to fake it! Faking confidence and control of the classroom may be necessary even though the reality is different. Displaying confidence can help to drastically reduce behavior problems, even if it is faked. Also, if teachers pretend that they are confident and in control for a long enough period of time, they will eventually begin to believe it. A little swagger goes a long way.

Someone Is Always Watching to See How Teachers Behave

Teaching is not a job that can be totally left at school at the end of the day. Teachers often have more responsibility than people in other professions. Even when away from school, teachers have a certain moral standard that they are expected to uphold. Getting tipsy or acting crazy in public does not look good. Some teachers have even lost their jobs for having pictures of themselves with a drink in their hand on their Facebook pages.

Even if there are no students around, there is no guarantee that there is not a parent, uncle, cousin, or someone else who may recognize the teacher even if they are far away from school. Teaching comes with a responsibility to be a positive example for young people, even after the school day is over. This may not seem fair, but it is a reality for teachers of all ages.

Every Student Cannot Be Saved

Sometimes new teachers have a "save the world" attitude when they first start their careers. Teaching is a noble profession, and those who are in it usually do a lot of good. Teachers may interact with many students who are headed down a bad road. There is no way to save every student, however. Sometimes influencing just one student is substantial. Also, many times teachers may not even get to see the impact they had. For some students, this impact may even be delayed. Sometimes these students may not even realize the positive influence their teachers had on them.

Sometimes the students who gave the teacher the most trouble are the ones who turn out to be the most positively affected. As a result, teachers cannot afford to tie their emotions to receiving gratitude from students. They just need to trust that they will have an impact in the long run, whether they get thanked or not.

TEACHER TIP
Give the Teaching Career Idea a Year or Two before Deciding to Give Up—Unless You Hate Every Minute of It

It is difficult to make a legitimate evaluation about teaching as a career choice after just one or two years in the profession. The usual thinking is that you do not really settle into a normal teaching routine until the third year. I remember some challenging classes I had during my first year of teaching. These were the kinds of classes that get shown in movies. It was so stressful and difficult that I made up my mind to quit about seven or eight times during the school year. I found out later that this experience is actually normal for many beginning teachers.

One time during that first year I even told an assistant principal that I quit. In his wisdom, he told me to go home during an upcoming break and think over my decision. I decided to stick it out, until the end of the school year. There were other times after that decision that I considered leaving, but now I am glad that I didn't. Eventually, I got much more comfortable in the job.

Some teachers may realize early on that teaching is not for them, and that is fine. If every minute of the job is a chore and you cannot wait to get home every day, then obviously it may not be the best career choice. My advice, though, is to stick it out for as long as possible, especially if there is any chance that it may work out in the long run. The sacrifice will be worth it.

Key Points

- New teachers should do all they can to reduce the difficulties that come with being new.
- Mentors can go a long way to making life easier for new teachers.
- Teaching is a calling, not just a job.
- The first day of school is especially important for new teachers to assert control and confidence.
- It is alright for new teachers to ignore some of the information they learned from their professors. This is especially true of the warning to "be mean at first and lighten up later."
- New teachers should figure out an efficient, organized grading style as quickly as possible.
- New teachers should be careful to have a separate life away from school.
- Saying yes to everything that is asked is a bad idea.
- All planning should be done at least one week in advance.
- A rewards system is not necessary outside of elementary school if an effective classroom management plan is in place.
- Every student cannot be saved. Having an impact on even one student makes the job worthwhile.
- New teachers should not give up on teaching if their first year or two is difficult.

12

Applying the Concepts of the New Style Plan to Parenting

How Poor Are They That Have Not Patience

> If you say you get along with your parents, well, you're a liar too.
>
> —from the movie *The Breakfast Club*

Even though the main focus of the New Style plan is on management in classrooms, many of the same principles can also be applied to raising children. There are differences in the two settings, of course, but finding a way to discipline children consistently is just as important for parents at home as it is for teachers at school.

The Age of Children Affects the Discipline Required

The age of the children involved is obviously an important factor for parents when developing discipline plans. Something that works for a five-year-old may not be appropriate for a sixteen-year-old. However, the general principles are usually the

---

Quoted from *Othello*.

same regardless of age. This is why each section in this chapter has an age designation in the heading.

Keys for Parents Using the New Style in the Home

1. Being Unemotional for Most Discipline Issues (All Ages)

Many parents want to use intimidation when trying to discipline their children. They think that meanness will get their children to behave. The problem with this strategy is that once parents establish this as their usual method, it is very difficult to make changes. This means that they are going to be stuck having to use this method every time they want to discipline their children. Do parents really want to have to be mean on a regular basis?

Another drawback to this method of discipline is that parents will likely have to get meaner and meaner for their actions to be effective. While meanness and intimidation may sometimes work in the short term, the end result will usually be conflict.

The best way to handle most situations where discipline is needed in the home is to be as matter-of-fact and unemotional as possible. This style shows children that their parents do not have a problem with them as people, only with their misbehavior. When anger is used to discipline, children sometimes feel their parents have an issue with them personally. Parents who can establish discipline without relying on emotion have a much better chance of having more cooperative and happy children.

2. Clearly Stating Rules and Consequences (All Ages)

Clarity of rules and consequences is important for children of all ages, but especially for younger ones. If rules and consequences are not clear, parents are left to make things up as they go. When parents make things up in this way, the results are often unfavorable. Parents will get much more respect and cooperation from their children when expectations are made clear. That way, when a child breaks a rule, the parent can just stay with the plan and implement the consequences. There is no room for the child to question, and there is no reason for the parent to get angry. The child then deals with the consequence and everyone moves on with little conflict. Beautiful.

3. Being Consistent and Committed (All Ages)

Consistency and commitment to a discipline plan may be the most important characteristic of successful parental discipline. If these things do not exist, it will not matter how brilliant the rules and consequences established are. Parents should decide what behaviors are acceptable and which ones are not, as well as what will happen if rules are broken. Also, they cannot afford to let some misbehaviors go unaddressed just because they are tired or because they do not feel like getting involved. This is why it is important for parents to take the job of choosing the rules and consequences seriously and to stay committed to whatever plan they choose.

Parents should only choose rules that they will be motivated to enforce. Also, both parents *must* agree on the rules and consequences that are being chosen. A lack of unity by parents can ruin any discipline plan. If parents get too ambitious and choose unrealistic rules or are not in agreement with every part of their plan, the result will be disastrous.

4. Keeping Public Records (Children Ages Ten and Under)

Having a posted list of rules and consequences can be very helpful, especially for children ages ten and under. This list helps both the parents and children have a constant reminder of the plan that has been established. Even the most conscientious parents can easily forget rules they have established without such a reminder. Getting the children involved in making a poster of the rules and consequences can also give them some ownership in the process. Having a posted list can also be a good way to keep a reminder of the progress that children make. Parents need to use every trick they can to try to keep their rules and consequences consistent. Having a posted sign displayed with all of the details shown clearly can be very helpful in achieving this goal.

5. Developing Reward Systems (Children Ages Ten and Under)

The use of a reward system is one of the few discipline strategies that can work better in the home than in the classroom. It can sometimes be very helpful for parents if they make their discipline plan like a game. When parents try to make the process fun this way, children will feel much more at ease about the process.

Rather than using anger and intimidation to implement rules in the home, parents can make it as if they are on the child's side *against* the discipline plan. When they do this, parents can then save the anger response for misbehaviors that are only very serious. If there are fun rewards in place for younger children for good behavior, they will often be much more motivated. Parents just need to be sure to *always* do what they say they are going to do when it comes to giving their children the rewards that were promised! Not following through with both rewards and punishments can ruin any discipline plan.

6. Using Repetition (All Ages)

Most parents realize that it takes repetition for children to learn something. As a result, parents should not be quick to get angry with their children if they break newly established rules. Parents should simply implement the consequence in a matter-of-fact way and move on. This style of implementing consequences should be used anyway in most cases, but it is especially true in the early stages of a new discipline plan when children are still learning the rules. Getting too harsh early on when children are still learning new rules can inspire rebellion.

7. Modeling the Appropriate Behavior (All Ages)

Modeling behavior is one of the most important things that parents do. Children learn the most from their parents by watching them. All of the talking and lip service about right and wrong is worthless if parents do not model the appropriate behavior themselves. From the time that children can talk, they pay more attention to what they see than what they hear. Parents who lecture all the time will often just get ignored anyway.

Parents who show character will inspire the same qualities from their children. This does not mean that parents should *never* talk about right and wrong. Children still need to hear about what they should and should not be doing. Parents should just not expect talking to solve all of their children's behavior issues. Also, just because they model good behavior is no guarantee that their children will automatically follow them. But, as a general rule, children will learn much more from their parents' actions than their parents' words. The old advice of "do what I say, not what I do" is useless.

8. Practicing Hypothetical Situations in the Beginning (Children Ages Ten and Under)

No matter what age children are, starting a new discipline plan could be difficult for them to get used to. It may also be true that even after the plan is implemented the children do not do anything to earn consequences for a while. As a result, it would be wise for parents to practice the way they want their plan to work. This practice should be done early on in the process, and may also be done later if the children behave so well that consequences are not needed for a while (not a bad problem to have!).

9. Using Both Criticism and Praise (All Ages)

Even if there is no formal plan in place, parents should always be aware of using a healthy balance of both praise and criticism with their children. Too much of either one is not productive. If too much criticism is used, children will feel like they cannot do anything right. If too much praise is used, they will feel like they cannot do anything wrong. Children do need to be praised often, but they also need to deal with the reality of knowing that sometimes they make mistakes that have consequences.

10. Not Issuing Severe Consequences in Front of Friends

One of the easiest ways for parents to get their children angry is to embarrass them in front of their friends. If children do something extreme, then parents may have no choice but to discipline them in public. When it comes to more minor infractions, however, parents can go a long way toward building a positive relationship with their children by waiting until the friends are gone to deal with consequences. This is one of the few times that it can be acceptable to not enforce a consequence immediately after a rule is broken. If parents feel that an immediate consequence is necessary, then they should at least be very careful to handle it in a matter-of-fact way to minimize the embarrassment.

11. Being Consistent with Siblings

Nothing gets children more angry than to think that they are not being treated as well as their siblings. Sometimes parents may act unfairly with different children in the family without even realizing it. Parents who want peace in their household, though, would be wise to make consequences as equitable as possible. This goal is much easier to accomplish when rules and consequences are clearly stated and displayed.

12. Not Trying to Be a Buddy (Children Ages Twelve and Up)

Parents of teenagers and preteens often want to be a buddy with their child. This may be acceptable for younger children, but definitely not older ones. Parents who get too buddy-buddy with older children will often lose their respect, as well as their ability to tell them no with any effect. These parents are afraid that they will lose popularity and often end up letting their teens do anything they want as a result.

Parents of older children are not just there to give advice; they should be in charge as well. Just being there as a friendly adviser is not good parenting. Parents should not hesitate to take a stand when they think it is necessary. They should also make it very clear that what they say goes in the household.

Once children are older and they move away, then parents can take the role of advice givers. Until then, however, the parents should be in charge.

Key Points

- The same principles used for the New Style of classroom management can also be used for parents' discipline plans at home.
- Parents should use an unemotional and matter-of-fact style when dealing with less serious misbehaviors.
- Rules and consequences should be clear and organized.
- Communication between parents and children about rules and consequences in the home is extremely important.
- Public record keeping of good and bad behavior can be very helpful to both parents and children.
- A reward system can be very helpful to parents, especially those who have younger children.
- Parents must model appropriate behavior if they really want to influence their children. Actions have much more impact than words.
- Parents should avoid mistakes that will turn their children against them. These mistakes may include not being fair among siblings, embarrassing children in front of friends, and not using enough praise.
- Being a buddy is not the job of parents. They should always be clearly in charge.

Conclusion

Parting Is Such Sweet Sorrow

> They ask me why I teach and I reply, "Where could I
> find such splendid company?"
>
> —John Wooden

There is a very real teacher emergency taking place. Our educational system as we know it is in a state of decline. There are
a lot of educators who have great teaching skills in their subject
areas but who do not have the minimum skills needed for successful classroom management. And a large number of skilled
people are not teaching at all; they have either left the profession or have not entered it in the first place because of a fear of
bad student behavior. The result of this loss of potentially great
teaching is that the quality of education that our children receive
is not nearly as good as it could be.

The good news is that the skills needed to be successful
with classroom management are not limited to a few naturally
gifted teachers. These skills can be learned! Yes, there are some
teachers who do have natural abilities for classroom management. However, these gifted teachers are by far the minority in

---

Quoted from *Romeo and Juliet*.

117

the profession. The only way to get our educational system to recover is to help those teachers who are not gifted with great classroom management skills to become competent. It is time our teachers learned how to get back into positions of power and control in their classrooms!

The goal of this book is to give teachers enough information to be able to learn these basic skills and to form a plan that fits their personalities. The New Style of classroom management works because it is simple and direct; it is reasonable to students, and it does not require massive amounts of paperwork.

There should not be a single student behavior in classrooms that teachers are not prepared to handle. The goal is not for teachers to be able to develop some utopian, perfectly run classroom. Rather, the goal is to get to a point where teachers no longer fear student misbehavior.

The reason for having rules and consequences is to set boundaries. Reasonable boundaries allow students to have an environment that maximizes their learning potential. Teachers should remember why they got into the profession in the first place. Hopefully, they entered it to help and serve students. Classroom management should be done with the best interest of children in mind. It should not just be done to punish or as an excuse to let out stress!

The key to reasonable discipline is to have the severity of consequences match the severity of misbehaviors. This idea is not rocket science. Students will rebel if they feel that they are not being treated fairly. The only chance that our schools have of reaching full potential is to operate with this approach in mind.

It is time that teachers stop relying on the old, less effective strategies of classroom management. Teachers can no longer afford to use anger and intimidation to accomplish their behavior management goals. Our schools are getting close to being in a state of emergency! The longer these behavior problems in schools go unsolved, the harder it will be to recover from them.

Imagine how much our schools would improve if the practice of classroom management was a smooth, relatively painless and stress-free process. Imagine if teachers did not have to worry about student misbehaviors, being free, instead, to use their creativity to teach at their highest levels. Without being burdened by the overwhelming stress that many teachers face today because of student misbehavior, schools would have a much better chance of helping their students reach their potential. And is that not what teaching is supposed to be about?

For more information, please visit my website at
www.withoutanger.com.

Appendix A

Frequently Asked Questions

Though This Be Madness, Yet There Is Method in It

> How'd they get you to stay? They gave me candy and called me their light.
>
> —from the movie *Dangerous Minds*

Can I Use the Five Minutes of Quiet Consequence for Extreme Situations?

The plan is not intended for extreme misbehavior. Most schools have plans in place for these occurrences anyway. 5 Minute Magic is made for minor situations that can still disrupt and even ruin a class if not taken care of. Extreme situations still deserve extreme reactions. The key is to not implement extreme consequences when student misbehaviors are not extreme.

Is It OK to Make Any Adjustments to the New Style Plans?

Yes, but be careful. Teachers should understand that the methods promoted in this book are not necessarily meant to be copied exactly. It is fine to have different rules and consequences

---

Quoted from *Hamlet*.

than the ones mentioned, but be careful to keep them appropriate. However, if adjustments to the New Style plans are made, they may not work as intended!

What If Students Cannot Make It to a Detention They Receive as a Consequence?

Students should be allowed to reschedule their detention one time with an acceptable excuse (given ahead of time). This is not made known to the students unless they ask. Also, if students say they have no way to stay after school for detention, tell them to make sure they don't get detention!

What Happens If Students Disrupt Class When They Get Up to Sign the Discipline Book for Breaking a Rule?

Some teachers may want students to sign their own name on a notebook or record of some kind when they receive a consequence. If this is the case, they must be totally quiet when they do so and show no reaction or they will move to the next step of consequences.

What Should I Do If a Student Regularly Gets Warnings but Rarely Goes Past That First Step of Consequences?

There may be a large number of students receiving consequences, especially early on. You must be willing to stick with your plan! Some students may push you to see if you are willing to follow through. Others may regularly try to get warnings and test your boundaries. If this happens, choose a number that is too many times to have received a warning in a given term (usually five). If they sign the book five times, for instance, start combining consequences for those students (i.e., after five consequences are given the students will get a five-minute dead quiet period and a one-minute detention). The same can be done for an entire class if they reach a certain number that the teacher feels is too many.

What Rules Are Appropriate to Use for the New Style?

This is one of the beauties of the plan. It is appropriate for any number of misbehaviors. There can be rules for somewhat minor offenses because the consequences are still reasonable. Feel free to modify this if necessary. However, do not have more than four steps on the consequences because this may cause the plan to become a burden for record keeping. The rules you choose should be for misbehaviors that get your attention when they are broken. For instance, if it does not really bother you when students tell each other to shut up, then do not include that in your rules.

How Many Rules and Consequences Should I Use?

Have as many or as few rules as seem reasonable, but generally no more than ten. The punishment will not be drastic at first so there can be consequences for any behavior that is undesirable, big or small. The students will usually not give you trouble about having stricter rules because the consequences will seem fair to them. This understanding eliminates the atmosphere of student against teacher in a classroom and promotes a much more positive atmosphere. This spirit of cooperation promotes more learning!

What If I Do Not Want to Be Bothered with Keeping Up with a Five-Minute Warning Period?

The five-minute period is useful but not a requirement for a successful plan. The more important idea for teachers is to find what is most comfortable for them. If a five-minute period of dead quiet is inconvenient, then choose another method.

What Can I Do to Get My Students Comfortable with the New Style?

I always try to find ways to demonstrate how the plan works early on in the term. I may do a little practice period where I give

124 / Appendix A

a consequence to the first person who talks. I may make it like a game and say that the loudest person in a certain time period will get a consequence. The key is to demonstrate your plan to the students early.

What If Students Claim That They Are Being Unfairly Punished or Did Not Know the Rule?

This is why the rules and consequences need to be posted and made as clear as possible. If it is on display, there is no excuse for not knowing the rule.

Can I Use the New Style in Homeroom or Other Nonteaching Situations?

Most definitely! The New Style is excellent for situations like homeroom, announcement time, going to the library, and so on. Even if teachers are not using the New Style as their main classroom management plan, they can still assign small consequences to handle these situations. Anything is better than having to rely on anger and making twenty requests to be quiet!

How Should I Handle Misbehaviors That Are Not Black and White, Such as Talking Too Much or Being Disrespectful?

Sometimes it is OK to use informal warnings that do not have a formal consequence associated with them. Try to get as specific as possible in these situations (see my earlier explanation of levels of volume that are allowed for different situations). Sometimes nonverbal communication such as a disapproving look can be effective. You might also make comments such as "you are getting close to being too loud."

Can I Stop Using the New Style Plan When My Classes Begin to Become Well Behaved?

Be careful about getting complacent when things seem to be going well. Students can behave for a while and then slip if you are not careful. I have seen classes behave dramatically differently in the first half of a semester compared with the second half because I took it for granted that they would continue to behave well on their own.

What If I Start to Fall Back to the Old Ways of Using Anger as a Tool for Handling Misbehavior?

Some habits are hard to break. Sometimes you have to remind yourself that you have a new, powerful plan now in place that does not require anger and intimidation. This is another benefit of having the rules and consequences posted in the classroom. The sign can serve as a good reminder for you too if you feel yourself slipping back into the old ways.

Appendix B

Ten Hypothetical Situations Using the New Style of Classroom Management

There should be no student misbehavior that happens in a classroom for which the teacher does not have an answer. Here are ten hypothetical situations and how they might be handled using the New Style plan for classroom management.

1. A Student Says Shut Up to Another Student

The "no shut up" rule is one that I am known for at my school. It is not a rule that would be easily enforced using traditional methods of classroom management. When a student says shut up to another student he must immediately go to the first step in the list of consequences that I have established for the class. This consequence is automatic with no room for debate. It does not matter if the student was kidding or not when he made the comment.

I have occasionally let a student get away with just saying the words "shut up" in a way that was not directed at another student. For instance, if she were doing something like telling someone about a time when somebody said the words to someone else, she would not earn a consequence. It is not the words being said that is forbidden; it is when they are directed at someone else. If students tell me to shut up, that is another issue, of course. The consequences would then be more severe.

This is the kind of rule that would not work using traditional methods of classroom management. Using the old methods, the teacher would have the choice of either getting angry whenever students used the phrase, or of overpunishing. The New Style plan allows for handling these more minor kinds of issues.

2. A Student Cusses under His Breath When Getting Back a Test

I have two separate rules for profanity in my class. The first rule is for swearing *at* someone. This is a serious issue. When this happens, I may remove the student from class, call administrators, parents, and so forth. This kind of behavior is not acceptable in a civilized classroom.

My second rule for profanity is for casual swearing. This means that the person used profanity that was not directed at another person. This could include things like swearing during a whispered conversation or a comment under one's breath when getting a bad grade on a test. When this happens, I assign an instant move to the second or third step on the list of consequences, which is a fifteen-minute detention after school (held in my classroom). This behavior is *not* immediate grounds for the most severe punishment available. Having to differentiate between levels of profanity does take a little more effort than just having one blanket rule, but it does allow for more fairness.

3. The Entire Class Is Talking Too Loudly

When a large number of students are talking loudly in class, it can be difficult for the teacher to select individuals who deserve consequences. In these situations, I will usually issue a class penalty of five minutes of dead silence. Any individual student who talks or whispers during this time would then move up the list of consequences established for the class. This includes talking to me, unless he has raised his hand or been called on. Very few questions are so pressing that they cannot wait five minutes to be asked.

4. The Class Is Being Introduced to the New Style Plan on the First Day of Class

On the first day of class, I like to go over my classroom management plan in detail. Communication and clarity when I am explaining my plan to students are very important. This is especially true since the students may not be familiar with my style of discipline. After I have discussed how the plan works, I will usually do a role-play scenario to show them what it looks like in a live situation. I may tell a student to act like she is in an argument, or to pretend to tell someone to shut up. Then we actually get to see what happens when a student has to go through the process of receiving a consequence and the procedures that go with the situation. Using a practice run is much better than having to explain everything again the first time that someone receives a consequence in a normal classroom situation.

5. A Student Talks during a Test or Quiz

For whatever reason, students always seem to want to talk at the end of tests when everyone is not quite finished. This issue was one of my most challenging discipline problems before I started using the New Style classroom management plan. Teachers who cannot keep a class quiet during test taking are not doing their job well.

The traditional answer for noncheating talking during tests is to give a failing grade on the test to the student who breaks the rule. The implication of this consequence is that the student's grade is severely affected, and therefore administration and parents are then involved. The problem with this course of action is that, in almost all cases, the students who break this rule are not cheating: they are simply getting restless. It becomes a classic case of mismatching severity. The severity of this punishment does not match the severity of the misbehavior.

My new strategy for handling talking at the end of tests is to issue a short group penalty of dead quiet time if it looks like students are beginning to talk or whisper at the end of tests. Students then move up my list of previously stated consequences if talking continues. Of course, if students are clearly talking about the test, a grade of zero would still be given. This plan just helps me avoid deciding whether or not to give a zero and make cheating accusations every time a student lets a word or two slip during a test.

When teachers plan to give a failing grade for talking of any kind during tests, they either overpunish students for non-cheating talking, or they let a lot go because of the fear of over-punishing. If classes make a habit of talking during tests, then something more severe may be in order. Otherwise, smaller consequences for occasional test-time talking are more appropriate.

6. Taking the Class to the Library

One of my favorite things to do when I am taking the class somewhere for a short period of time (library, computer lab) is to play a little game involving my discipline plan. Keeping students orderly outside of the classroom can be even more difficult than it is inside the classroom. Therefore, I will tell the class that we are going to have a competition. Whoever is the loudest from the time that we leave the room until the time we return will get a penalty (usually the lowest penalty that I have in my plan—five minutes of dead silence). It is a totally relative situation. As part of the game, students could possibly get a consequence for things that would not normally result in one in the usual classroom setting (i.e., if everyone behaved well and one person slipped and barely talked).

I tell the class that it is possible to have a tie between multiple students in this competition, and that it is also possible to have no loser if the class is perfect. I have had both of those situations occur when I have done this exercise. The great thing about this exercise is that the classes almost always behave extremely well, even better than would usually be expected. None of the students want to lose the competition, and this motivates them.

This activity often works so well that the librarians and other teachers who witness it are often blown away by the great behavior of the students. It definitely beats having to say "shush!" a hundred times and being stressed out every time you have to take a class out in public!

7. A Student Breaks My Rule against General Incivility

I always have a rule in my classes that there will be "no general incivility" allowed. The reason for this rule is that students somehow come up with uncivilized behaviors that have never occurred to me. They obviously should not be allowed to get away with their behavior if it is not appropriate for a civilized class. Therefore, I include this rule to cover any of the surprising misbehaviors that students might come up with during the course of a school year.

When a student behaves in a way that I might think is uncivilized but is not covered in my rules, I try to handle it in a matter-of-fact way. For instance, suppose a student came in and started making loud burping noises. Do I have a specific rule forbidding burping in class? No, I would have never thought to include this rule in my list. If I do not want this behavior taking place, though, I need to have something planned ahead of time to allow me to be able to handle this situation.

My usual response when a student behaves in a way that might be considered uncivilized would be to say something like "I think that might be in the generally uncivilized category. Don't you think?" Or I might ask the class the same question. I try to make it clear that I am not trying to trick them or trap them into being punished. In almost all cases, either the student or the class will agree that the behavior was uncivilized as I suggested.

If the student can give me a good reason why the behavior was not uncivilized, I may consider letting her get away with just an informal warning. If I decide, however, that the behavior is too uncivilized to allow, I will give some kind of consequence even if the class disagrees. The consequence will almost always be the first step on my list of consequences, which will be something light like five minutes of dead silence. Since the consequence is less severe, I usually do not get much argument, even if the student feels as if she did not deserve any punishment for the behavior. I do at least try to give students some chance to defend themselves.

If you do not have a rule like "no general incivility" included in your classroom management plan, you are opening yourself up for students to respond with the "it's not one of your rules so how can I be punished for it?" defense. Including this rule allows you to have a reasonable answer to that question because there is no misbehavior that cannot be covered. Since a major cause of stress for teachers is the fear of having unexpected student misbehavior and not knowing how to respond, this rule can be a great way to reduce that problem.

8. Two Students Start Arguing in Class

Sometimes students get into arguments in the middle of class. When this happens, it can be difficult for a teacher to decide how to handle the situation. Many times students may be raising their voices when this happens and even acting as if they are about to fight. If the teacher is not prepared to deal with this kind of situation ahead of time, it may be difficult to react with a reasonable response. Should the students be removed from class? Should they be sent into the hallway for a private discussion with the teacher? Should a battle of raised voices take place until the teacher shouts them down? None of these possibilities are good ideas.

Student arguing is an issue that is best to discuss with students ahead of time. I might include raising voices as part of the general incivility rule discussed earlier, or I may have a more specific rule about arguing. A problem that could occur is trying to define what exactly falls into the category of arguing. Also, a "no arguing" rule might be too vague to enforce consistently. My answer to student arguing is to have a rule about raising voices and to take the students out of the room immediately if they do so. From that point I can then decide if they have done anything to deserve further consequences. They will likely receive at least a minimum consequence for the behavior if it gets to that point, however.

9. A Student Tries to Eat or Drink Something in Class When It Is Not Allowed

I have always had a "no food or drink" rule in my classroom. My answer to this issue used to be that I would take food and drinks away and throw them out immediately. I quickly found, though, that students sometimes get *very* upset when teachers do this! Some of them may feel as if the teacher is stealing from them when this occurs, since they just paid for the drink or food. I have seen students respond with intense anger and hatred when I have thrown food and drinks away.

I realize that I could probably get away with continuing this practice, especially if I told the students about it ahead of time. However, I have decided that this is not a battle worth fighting. My new policy is to take the food or drink away from students but give it back to them at the end of the period. A lot of times, students forget to retrieve their food or drink at the end of the period anyway. When this happens, I end up throwing it out like I normally would have in the first place. All teachers have to choose the battles that they want to fight. This is not one that I worry too much about.

10. Students Get Out of Their Seats before the Bell Rings

If students in my classes get out of their seats even one second before the bell rings, the individual students who broke the rule have to stay after class for a one-minute detention. The detention requires staying seated for the entire minute. I have never had this happen so many times that I had to keep a record of it for repeat offenders, but if it became a problem I might determine a maximum number of times (such as five) before I would start assigning afterschool detention for the repeaters. There is just something about gathering up at the door before the bell rings that encourages mischief for students. I would rather just eliminate the practice by not allowing them out of their seats at all until the bell actually rings. Those teachers using this rule should be sure to start from day one. Changing this rule in the middle of the term can be more difficult than it would be for other rules.

Appendix C

Ladder of Consequences Form

Ladder of Consequences
(Keep it simple.)

Teacher: _____

Class: _____

Semester: _____

DATE	NAME	TIME	CHECKS	# Days name was written down

Index